LITERACY LIBRARIES AND LEARNING

Using books and online resources to promote
reading, writing, and research

EDITORS
RAY DOIRON
MARLENE ASSELIN

Pembroke Publishers Limited

© 2005 Pembroke Publishers
538 Hood Road
Markham, Ontario, Canada L3R 3K9
www.pembrokepublishers.com

Distributed in the U.S. by Stenhouse Publishers
480 Congress Street
Portland, ME 04101-3400
www.stenhouse.com

We acknowledge the financial support of the Government of Canada through the Book Publishing Industry Development Program (BPIDP) for our publishing activities.

We acknowledge the support of the Government of Ontario through the Ontario Media Development Corporation Book Fund.

Library and Archives Canada Cataloguing in Publication

Doiron, Ray, 1949-
   Literacy, libraries and learning : using books to promote reading, writing, and research / Ray Doiron and Marlene Asselin.

Includes index.
ISBN 1-55138-196-6

   1. Language arts (Elementary). 2. Exposition (Rhetoric)—Study and teaching (Elementary). 3. Library orientation—Study and teaching (Elementary). I. Asselin, Marlene, 1949- II. Title.

LB1575.8.D665 2005   372.6   C2005-905684-3

Editor: Kate Revington
Cover Design: John Zehethofer
Typesetting: JayTee Graphics

Printed and bound in Canada
9 8 7 6 5 4 3 2

Contents

Using Children's Books

Using Online Learning Resources

Biographies of Chapter Contributors

Angela Arsenault has been an elementary school classroom teacher and teacher-librarian for more than 10 years. She has training in school librarianship through the University of Prince Edward Island and recently earned her Masters in Education degree. Her thesis centred on the collaborative planning process. Angela has presented her research at conferences and has taken part in library and professional development committees in Prince Edward Island.

Richard Beaudry has been a public school teacher for more than 20 years in immersion and francophone schools in Alberta and British Columbia. Since 1987, he has worked as a teacher-librarian in British Columbia. He has also worked as a reference librarian for that province's Ministry of Education. Richard's research interests pertain to technology integration in school libraries and standards of information literacy skills taught in collaboration with classroom teachers.

Dr. Margot Filipenko is a faculty member in the Department of Language and Literacy Education at the University of British Columbia. Earlier, she taught young children for 15 years. Her research interests focus on young children's development in information literacy.

Elizabeth A. Lee is an assistant professor of language and literacy in the Faculty of Education, Queen's University, Canada. She taught elementary school in Winnipeg for 20 years before becoming a professor. Her research interests are instruction in reading, information literacy, and adolescent literacy. She teaches graduate and teacher education courses in cognition, reading, and language arts.

Keith McPherson has been a teacher and teacher-librarian in private and public schools, in both rural and urban British Columbia settings since 1983. Now the director of the Department of Language and Literacy Education Research Centre, he runs professional development programs for preservice and inservice teachers wishing to learn how to integrate technologies and information literacy into language arts classrooms and school libraries.

Lyndsay Moffatt is an elementary teacher-librarian with the Toronto District School Board and a doctoral student at the University of British Columbia. Before becoming a teacher she worked for 10 years at a bookstore that specialized in progressive children's books. She thanks the students at Givins/Shaw school for teaching her that even young children can understand issues of fairness and civil rights. She thanks her principal Janet Duffy for supporting her efforts to create a more tolerant school.

Introduction

Classroom Teachers and Teacher-Librarians Working Together as Champions for Literacy

Ray Doiron and Marlene Asselin

Literacy programs have traditionally relied on school libraries to supply books and reference materials for students' independent reading and for completion of research reports. Regardless of the approach to teaching literacy, classroom teachers sent children for library books and encouraged them to read. When a social studies or science unit required a research project, students often used an encyclopedia, several non-fiction trade books, and some audio-visual resources to complete their projects. The teacher-librarian primarily distributed and managed library resources and taught "library skills," usually in isolation from the classroom program. We understood that the purpose of a school library was mainly to provision classroom programs.

Several factors have combined to change the relationship between school library and classroom-based literacy programs; they also raise our awareness that both programs play a role in children's literacy achievement.

First of all, resources have changed and broadened dramatically. A school library still maintains a solid collection of fiction and easy reading (picture) books, as well as a wide range of the latest information books. Information books, though, have changed in character. They have gone from the dull and dreary texts of bygone times to comprehensive, visual treasures that lure students into a wide variety of contemporary subjects. With innovations in digital technologies have come many new types of resources, too. These include Web-based static sites and more interactive, virtual learning environments. All this has heightened the need for more expertise in selecting and accessing these resources; it has also called for instructional leadership on the part of the teacher-librarian to integrate these resources into teaching and learning.

In addition to changes in school library resources, the nature of classroom literacy programs has changed. These have become structured around children's literature, both fiction and information books. Effective teaching of a literature-based program relies on a greater and richer collection of resources than a single classroom could possibly have. When teachers want to give a direct instruction lesson on rhyming words, adjectives, or one of myriad writing skills, they seek out strong examples from children's books which will connect their lessons to the reading students will do. This approach highlights the need for classroom teachers and teacher-librarians to communicate more as they try to connect resources to instruction.

Teachers also seek to reflect our multicultural world in their literacy programs. They search for representative materials that create richness and diversity in their instructional programs. The task can be daunting, though, as they try to be as inclusive as possible and to address many concerns and issues. Supporting a school library allows a school to build a larger and more diverse collection of resources that represent all people in the local and world communities. The library becomes a dynamic resource shared equally by all teachers.

Another factor in strengthening the relationship between teacher-librarians and classroom teachers is the growing and pervasive influence of information and communication technologies (ICT). School libraries have traditionally been home to many "information technologies," such as filmstrips, videos, and sound recordings, but the Internet has eliminated most of those resources; instead, it has made online digital resources and online learning environments key components in most standards-based curriculum frameworks. Classroom teachers, now expected to integrate ICTs into teaching and learning, need the help of a specialist, like the teacher-librarian, to meet these growing expectations.

The Internet has also raised all sorts of questions about selecting appropriate digital resources and providing all students with equitable access to resources—it heightens the importance of teaching critical literacy. With their expertise in ICTs and knowledge of the skills and strategies associated with finding and using information, teacher-librarians stand as essential players and effective partners in developing any school curriculum.

With such a vast array of exciting and innovative resources at their disposal, classroom teachers and teacher-librarians have all the tools to provide effective literacy instruction and improve student achievement; however, effective teaching is not enough. Many forces compete for children's attention and interests, so teachers and teacher-librarians have become *champions for literacy*, promoting and encouraging reading in every aspect of their work. Teachers and teacher-librarians have always been avid readers and promoters of reading for their students. In today's highly technological world, though, it is essential that we *combine* our efforts and make reading—and literacy in general—the number one priority for our schools.

We have all heard teachers complain that students do not read enough or that some just do not enjoy it. We can no longer dismiss such comments, if we ever could. Instead, if we find that students do not like to read, an alarm bell should sound in our ears. The news should goad us to action. All of the time, we need to use all the ways we possibly can to motivate students to read, to help them develop the reading habit, to provide them with time and resources for reading to happen at school. We need to model the power that reading has in *our* lives, to show students that we read too, in other words, to persuade them that in their lives, they need to make reading a priority.

1

Redefining the School Library's Role in Literacy Teaching and Learning

Marlene Asselin

This chapter recognizes the great potential influence of school library programs in students' educational success. Observations, such as those below, point to this awareness which offers educators hope in meeting students' literacy needs.

"Researchers show more and more evidence of the key role in student achievement for well stocked and well staffed libraries."

Reading Today,
February–March 2003, p. 1

"Libraries served as a major resource for homework help in poor neighborhoods . . . at times there were crowds requiring security guards to only allow children to come in when someone would leave."

Susan Neumann, 2001, n.p.

The connection between libraries and literacy may seem intuitive; however, the specific ways that school library programs can support literacy teaching and learning in schools is less known to educators. As understood in this book, **school library programs** consist of the units of study developed through the shared expertise and equal partnership of classroom teachers and teacher-librarians; based on the principles of resource-based learning, these are designed to achieve the educational goals of the school.

This chapter reviews current research about the effects of school library programs on teaching and learning. It outlines the conditions that need to be in place for school library programs to best enrich literacy education; it also describes four major ways in which the teacher-librarian directly affects literacy teaching and learning. When teachers understand how teacher-librarians contribute to teaching and learning, they can promote literacy much more effectively.

The Case That Research Makes

The central place of libraries in learning communities has been understood since medieval times. Much literacy research confirms that when students have access to a wide and rich range of literature and information resources, their literacy development is significantly enhanced. (*Access for All*, by Neumann, Celano, Greco & Shue, is an example.) Whether in our homes, communities, or school libraries, investments in print and electronic resources signal that literacy and learning are valued. Librarians know how to develop, maintain, and use these collections. They help others access what they want or need, introduce resources that a person may not otherwise find, build a collection of resources tailored to readers' needs and preferences, and teach others how to gain access to what they need.

How School Libraries Benefit Literacy and Learning

The wider educational community is now aware of research that has been building for decades. Across countries, the important place of school libraries in improving students' reading abilities and their love of reading is well documented. Recent international literature reviews and large-scale studies have confirmed the role of school libraries in teaching and learning, specifically related to academic and reading achievement, and the fostering of pleasure in reading and learning.

In the United States, a program of state-wide investigations has focused on the relationship of school libraries to student gains (Keith Curry Lance's *ERIC Digest* article, "Proof of the Power," provides an overview of this program). Some states have undertaken their own studies. For example, in Texas it was found at all educational levels that scores for the state assessment tests were higher in schools with librarians than in those without (Smith, 2001). And in Iowa, the highest achieving students came from schools with high-quality school libraries (as determined by resources, staffing, and integration with school curriculum) (Rodney, Lance, & Hamilton-Pennell, 2002).

In Ohio, Ross Todd and Carol Kuhlthau have explored the role of school libraries in student learning by talking directly with students. In stage one of the Ohio Educational Library Media Association project, interview responses from more than 13,000 students revealed the many ways that teacher-librarians affect their reading and learning. These comments focus on three key ways:

1. *Teacher-librarians connect books with readers.*

   "I like to read books about creepy things and the library lady has given me the words to use to find them in the computer."

   "When I couldn't find a cool book that I would be interested in, the librarian helped me find a science fiction book. I now read a lot more science fiction and my mommy is proud!"

2. *Teacher-librarians instruct students in identifying and locating relevant information for research assignments.*

   "When I needed help with my projects (no matter what class it was for), they helped me figure out what I was doing, and what I needed to find out, and where I needed to go."

   "I had to write a term paper on abortion and had no clue about what sites were good to look for information. They helped me with finding good sites that really helped with the project, such as opposing points of view."

3. *Teacher-librarians provide students with strategies for learning from sources.*

   "I didn't really know how to do reading and I was getting bad grades then we started doing main idea reading which we learned in library classes. Now I know how to do main idea and put my other ideas around it."

Comprehensive reviews of the research on the influence of school libraries on learning have also been done in Canada (Haycock, 2003), Australia (Lonsdale, 2001), and Scotland (William, Wavell, & Cole, 2001). These reviews synthesize the research that affirms the role of access to resources and skilled librarians. They deal with the following three dimensions of education:

- *Learning in the content areas.* Students learn better when they have free access to the school library, know how to use the library's information sources, and are taught how to read, organize, and communicate what they are learning with help from teacher-librarians.
- *Reading literacy achievement.* Students can improve their reading abilities when school library programs are designed to enable them to choose from a rich collection of texts, to be exposed to new titles and genres, and to spend time reading on a school-wide reading basis.
- *Positive feelings about reading and learning.* When teacher-librarians model and celebrate the power of reading with students and connect them with meaningful books, students become more motivated to read, view reading favorably, and see themselves as readers. When teacher-librarians help students learn how to independently locate and evaluate information, read for main ideas, and share learning in a variety of modes, students feel more confident in their reading abilities and better see themselves as lifelong learners.

In sum, research from both the literacy and library fields indicates that teacher-librarians, through their collections and programs, can build on classroom instruction in multiple ways: from providing access to reading material to supporting students through the complex processes of research.

Factors That Affect the Development of a School Library Program

Knowing the potential contributions of school library programs to literacy and learning begs the question of how these programs can be developed. Not all school libraries have the ideal conditions and structures, as identified by research, to fully nurture literacy and learning. These factors relate to

- funding and administrative matters, specifically collection levels, library staffing levels, and collaboration between teacher-librarian and teachers
- teachers' understanding of the role of the teacher-librarian and the school library program.

Funding and Administrative Matters

Three major policy practices influence the degree to which school libraries can make a difference in teaching and learning in our schools.

1. *Hiring qualified (full-time) staff.* **Teacher-librarians** are specialist educators with additional qualifications in curriculum, literacy, administration, and information literacy, or the abilities to locate and use information to learn. The International Reading Association (2000) recognizes that "credentialed school library media professionals promote, inspire, and guide students toward a love of reading, a quest for knowledge, and a thirst for lifelong learning." Many school systems in both Canada and the United States, though, have severely reduced

school library staff positions, replaced teacher-librarians with technicians, or assigned large chunks of the teacher-librarian's schedule to provide classroom teachers with "prep time."

2. *Building a rich and current collection of literature and information resources that includes school-wide networking to library resources.* The role of access in literacy development is well established in both the literacy and library communities. For example, a 1999 position statement by the International Reading Association affirms: "Without appropriate access to books, children will be taught to read but will not develop the habit of reading . . . Children who have access to books are more likely to read for enjoyment and information. Children who read for enjoyment increase their reading skills and their desire to read to learn" (p. 2). Also, research by Topping and others concludes: "Since performance was associated with access to reading materials and cultural artifacts, schools should work to ensure that all students are surrounded in their classrooms, school libraries and elsewhere by new, interesting and diverse reading materials, and teachers should facilitate access to these materials" (2003, p. 12).

Literature and information-rich environments can increase what students learn, how widely they read, and how much they read. In a study of reading in 32 countries, differences between high- and low-scoring countries included well-stocked school and classroom libraries and higher frequency of book borrowing (Froese, 1997). In the U.S. project, Library Power, schools received funding to improve their school library collections, and these improvements were correlated to students' increased academic achievement (Zweizig & Hopkins, 1999).

What is a healthy school library collection? As *Achieving Information Literacy* documents for school libraries in Canada, specific guidelines are available from library associations. The International Reading Association (1999) outlines the main principles of developing a strong print collection:

- Libraries ensure that there is a fair balance between children who receive access to books outside of school and those who do not.
- Libraries purchase new books each year, the number of which is determined by the school population, and make a concentrated effort to replace older materials for each classroom and school library annually. (For print resources, a rule of thumb is that at least 35 books per child are needed as a base collection, with the addition of two new titles per year per child; see *Achieving Information Literacy* by Asselin, Branch, & Oberg.)
- Libraries include storybooks, novels, biographies, nonfiction, magazines, poetry, and other types of print materials to suit the interests and reading abilities of all children.

3. *Structuring time so that teachers and teacher-librarians can collaboratively plan and teach.* Library resources need to be integrated into the school curriculum and students need to be taught how to use them effectively to learn. These things cannot happen in isolation. Gone are the days of "library skills" instruction while the teacher is off somewhere else. Teachers and teacher-librarians may use a curriculum development process called Collaborative Program Planning and Teaching (CPPT).

Using the CPPT model, they plan and teach resource-based units grounded in core curriculum. They also address the skills and strategies that students need if they are to use a wide range of learning resources effectively (see *Partners in Learning* by Doiron & Davies for many ideas). Chapter 2 will closely examine the CPPT process.

Finding *time* to collaborate can be next to impossible. The wise administrator fosters a culture for collaboration in the school by allotting time, which, in turn, nurtures the potential for higher use of learning resources and for increased student learning.

Especially in today's context of diversity, both adequate funding and strong administrative support of school libraries are essential. An examination of school libraries in a large U.S. city found

> Despite similarities in budget allocations, there were striking differences in the quality of school libraries . . . Children in poor areas had mediocre to poor libraries, no librarian on site; further the libraries were often closed during the week, compared to those in middle-class schools in the same city. School library funds were designated as discretionary to be used for computers if the instructional leader chose to do so. Thus, many of these schools in poor areas had no libraries, but computer labs, often empty of anything but the technology itself (Neumann, 2001).

These findings are corroborated by a 1993 study of Colorado school libraries. In *The Impact of School Library Media Centers on Academic Achievement*, Lance, Welborn, and Hamilton-Pennell noted, "Students at schools with better funded LMCs (Library Media Centers) tended to achieve higher average reading scores, whether their schools and communities are rich or poor and whether adults in the community are well or poorly educated."

Teacher Understandings

The quality of teacher and teacher-librarian collaboration depends on shared understandings of the role of the teacher-librarian and of the school library program. Older notions of the school library as a warehouse, the teacher-librarian as a strict resource manager, and the instructional focus of the school library as "library skills" block the creation of dynamic partnerships.

Limited notions about school libraries persist, however. Reviews of teacher education programs in both Canada and the United States reveal that little is being done to show new teachers how to use the programs and services of school libraries. In 2003, Marlene Asselin and Ray Doiron reported that many classroom teachers tend to equate information literacy with older notions of library or research skills. (See page 65 for an accurate definition of what it means to be information literate.) Classroom teachers also have undeveloped understandings about how to effectively plan **resource-based learning**, which actively involves students, teachers, and teacher-librarians in the effective use of a wide range of print, non-print, and human resources; in this type of learning, students "approach a theme, issue or topic of study in ways which allow for a range of learning styles and access to the theme or topic via cognitive or affective appeals" (PEI Building Information Literacy at http://www.edu.pe.ca/bil/bil.asp?ch1.s2.gdtx). Furthermore, they are unsure about the role of the school library program in student learning (Asselin, 2001; Moore, 2000). One U.S. study of how often teacher-librarians and classroom teachers collaborate for information literacy instruction found that only 15–20 percent of elementary and secondary teachers team-teach with teacher-librarians, and only 11 percent of those teacher-librarians do so regularly (Whelan, 2003).

Teachers play a critical role in enabling the potential of school library programs to be realized. Fully integrated school library programs rely on teachers' knowledge of how teacher-librarians support the development of information literacy, how school library collections and programs pass on cultural heritage, how information technologies can assist learning, and how school libraries act as community access points for teachers and students.

Effective models of how to introduce new teachers to school library programs have been developed in three Canadian universities. These teacher education models get new teachers working directly with teacher-librarians in their literacy methods courses and in their practicum schools. The teacher-librarians mentor the new teachers by helping them develop resource-based units of instruction, and planning and teaching information literacy lessons. Classroom teachers can learn about school libraries by attending professional development events that focus on information literacy, resource-based learning, and collaborative teaching, and by meeting with the teacher-librarian in their school to plan ways to work together to support literacy and learning.

The Roles the Teacher-Librarian Can Play to Strengthen Literacy

Each school needs to develop its own rationale and vision for the school library's role in meeting learning outcomes for literacy. The teacher-librarian may promote the library's role at staff meetings and among staff members and build on collaborative experiences to bring the library's role to people's attention. The more fully integrated the school library becomes with the classroom literacy program, the more effective literacy learning will be. The more teachers develop shared goals for their school library, and understand how the teacher-librarian can help them promote literacy and teach information literacy, the better able a school can support students' literacy development—of course, classroom libraries contribute to this effort, as well. Schools are wise to recognize the role of the school library and the teacher-librarian in their school improvement initiatives and to articulate the role of a teacher-librarian.

Four major roles of the teacher-librarian directly affect the quality of literacy education and learning in a school:

- providing access to curricular-based resources that improve teaching and learning

- promoting reading
- teaching the literacy skills needed for finding and using information
- collaborating with teachers in planning, teaching, and evaluating literacy

Teachers who understand these roles and enable their teacher-librarian to play them can strengthen their students' literacy development. These roles should be considered when a school sets out to envision the part that its school library and teacher-librarian can play.

Providing Access to Curricular-based Resources That Improve Teaching and Learning

The many benefits of a rich selection of resources have already been discussed. Today's library collections are designed to

- support the curriculum
- support students' independent reading
- serve as a portal to resources out of the school 24 hours a day, seven days a week
- offer accessibility before, during, and after school for print materials, not just at weekly "book exchange" times, and to the school library catalogue and all its resources from any computer in the school or out

Examples of award-winning school library sites can be found at **http://www.iasl-slo.org/ web_winners.html**.

The teacher-librarian consults with teachers and students about desired new resources. Teachers advise the teacher-librarian of topics and perspectives that students will learn; online, in class, or on a page in the library, students recommend titles, genres, and topics they are interested in. Teacher-librarians have special training in selecting resources. They know a wide market of suppliers, keep current with new print and electronic resources, and know how to organize resources so they can be accessed easily. Most school libraries now have their own Web sites where teachers and students can gain ready access to a variety of resources tailored to the curriculum. These customized Web sites include other features such as tutorials, links to local libraries, professional resources, and a student gallery which showcases students' favorite books and their best work. (See Chapter 6 for more on school library Web sites.)

Promoting Reading

Literacy promotion strategies will be discussed in detail in Chapter 3.

Promoting reading fosters a love and habit of reading in students, and when students love reading, they will choose to read more and their reading achievement will be greater. Students who are "turned on" to reading learn about the world as well as develop their reading abilities which, in turn, enable them to read increasingly complex texts. This truth points to the critical activity of "getting the right book in the right child's hands" so that it stays there, not just momentarily but long enough for the child to become fully engaged with the text. Teacher-librarians are, first of all, readers themselves—reading is in the blood. They have a wide repertoire of strategies for exposing students to new titles, authors, and genres.

Their passion, their promotion strategies, and their access to a rich and diverse collection combine to help hook students on reading and on coming to know the lifelong pleasure reading can bring.

Teaching the Literacy Skills Needed for Finding and Using Information

Current visions of education are rooted in goals of lifelong learning and a learning society. For example, in one definition, education is "a lifelong learning process where educators strive to create a learning society in which the acquisition, renewal, and use of knowledge is cherished" (see Council of Ministers of Education, Canada, 1999). What it means to be literate is expanding to reflect these new values and the infusion of information and communication technologies (ICT) into our everyday lives and workplaces. A recent international study of students' reading abilities stated that literacy researchers foresee that, in the future, literacy will include fluent information retrieval and processing.

One aspect of emerging definitions of literacy entails what teacher-librarians call **information literacy**, the abilities to locate, analyze, and communicate information. For example, literacy researchers Leu, Kinzer, Coiro & Cammack (2004, p. 1572) state that "new literacies allow us to use the Internet and other ICTs to identify important questions, locate information, critically evaluate the usefulness of that information, synthesize information to answer those questions, and then communicate the answers to others." Researchers who are examining the impact of new technologies on literacy have determined that students need help learning how to search and locate information on the Internet, comprehend **hypermediated text**, or Internet text that is composed of multiple links, and critically evaluate online information. These abilities, integral components of the school library program, aim to move teachers from developing traditional research projects focused on facts to developing new knowledge and new understanding.

The focus on information literacy and its applications in the "new literacies" means that students make inquiries based on thoughtful questions and use the knowledge they gain to take social action, make informed decisions, and solve problems. For example, using many diverse resources, students may research the issues and perspectives pertinent to a debate in their community: perhaps a vacant lot is being considered for residential development or viewed as a potential park in a densely populated area. Their reports and recommendations could be posted on the school library Web site and even presented at a city council meeting.

Learning outcomes are beginning to include these aspects of literacy, but school library programs have already developed systematic curricula of information literacy extending from core curriculum and drawing from existing curriculum. (See, for example, Ontario Library Association, 1999; Washington Library Media Association, 1996; Prince Edward Island Department of Education, 2001.) Teacher-librarians have special training in teaching information literacy. When teachers and teacher-librarians combine efforts to help students learn these new literacies, it is in context of curriculum-based units of inquiry in any subject area. The chart below displays the way teacher-librarians organize instruction of information literacy.

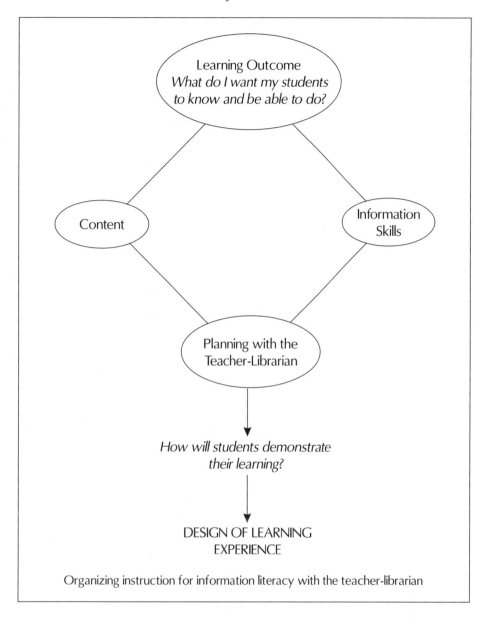

Learning Outcome
What do I want my students to know and be able to do?

Content

Information Skills

Planning with the Teacher-Librarian

How will students demonstrate their learning?

DESIGN OF LEARNING EXPERIENCE

Organizing instruction for information literacy with the teacher-librarian

Together, the teacher-librarian and teacher develop a resource-based approach to students' learning. Learning resources are selected to ensure diversity and variety in mode, perspective, and reading level. The teacher and teacher-librarian plan specific information skills to teach students and have them practise in context during the unit. Regular collaboration with the teacher-librarian means that learning outcomes for information literacy will be systematically addressed for each class. It also means that there will be a logical progression from one year to the next as students advance through the grades.

Collaborating with Teachers in Planning, Teaching, and Evaluating Literacy

Collaboration is the heart of the teacher-librarian's role. Unless classroom teachers recognize this, though, the teacher-librarian cannot properly fulfill the role. Just as being a judge depends on having someone to judge, the ability of the teacher-librarian to serve depends on teachers' willingness to collaborate. Without many types and levels of partnership with teachers, the potential impact of the school library on the quality of teaching and learning is diminished.

Teachers may collaborate with teacher-librarians

- to schedule booktalks
- to extend classroom instructional resources
- to design learning activities and projects
- to teach information skills
- to get teaching ideas and suggestions for learning resources
- to plan and teach content-area units
- to create learning stations where students can work independently
- to teach the legal and ethical uses of information and ideas

Conversely, teachers can use the school library in these ways:

- as a place where students are taught specific research or information skills and strategies by the teacher-librarian
- as a place for students to find information
- as a work space for the whole class, a small group, or individuals
- as a place for teachers and students to access information and communication technologies (e.g., video, computer, television)
- as a place to share and present students' work

These lists of ideas demonstrate that a school library is much more than a storage facility for books and audio-visual materials. They also point to the need for it to be staffed with a qualified teacher-librarian who can build that collection of learning resources into a vital and rich part of literacy programs.

Schools need to envision the school library as part of the whole school plan for achieving full literacy for all students. The school library program develops when teachers and teacher-librarians actively plan, teach, and evaluate units of study with information literacy a strong focus of the collaboration. It is energized by a mutual love of literacy and a desire to nurture a passion for literacy throughout students' lives. Teacher-librarians are prepared and trained to be full partners in literacy education. What schools need to ensure is that they are given the opportunity.

2

Developing a Full Literacy Partnership

Ray Doiron and Angela Arsenault

Since they are knowledgeable in all areas of the curriculum, the integration of various resources into the curriculum, the promotion of reading, and the development of information literacy, teacher-librarians can be valuable partners in developing students' learning. Already, they provide leadership within school library programs, and by forming partnerships with classroom teachers, they can extend this leadership to the development and teaching of various aspects of the literacy program.

Introducing a Process

In many cases, the teacher-librarian introduces a process for collaboration. Soon, though, classroom teachers see the benefits and call on the teacher-librarian to attend grade-level and other planning sessions.

The model likely to be introduced is the Collaborative Program Planning and Teaching (CPPT) process. This process, outlined clearly in *Partners in Learning: Students, Teachers and the School Library*, focuses on developing student-centred activities that engage students in learning and encourage them to be independent, lifelong learners. It also helps them develop positive reading habits. As partners, teachers and teacher-librarians develop curriculum that integrates resources, information skills, and shared program objectives.

The CPPT process may be used for a variety of instructional planning activities. It enables teachers and teacher-librarians to plan the teaching of traditional research skills, use of information sources, use of information and communication technologies (ICT), and the many information skills needed by information literate people. When teachers and teacher-librarians work together, students learn to search efficiently, to skim and scan a text for information, to take notes, to avoid plagiarizing, to make effective presentations, and more. Also, motivating and encouraging students to read becomes a shared responsibility between the classroom and the school library; this partnership has greater impact on student learning when individual teachers or grade levels work with the teacher-librarian to pool ideas, share resources, and create a unified curriculum for student learning.

The teacher-librarian, as part of meeting school library goals, may set planning times, show classroom teachers where they could easily work together, and model how the process works and what the many benefits are when teachers work together for student learning.

The Points of Connection between Classrooms and School Libraries

It is one thing to propose that teachers and teacher-librarians plan and teach together, but often this question arises: *What* are they going to teach together? What areas of the curriculum make for the most natural connection between classrooms and school libraries? Let's take an example and examine how the two connect.

Two Grade 4 teachers are beginning a new thematic unit on Canada and the World. More than 45 students will be learning about aspects of other countries, such as economy, education system, family life and recreation, and comparing/contrasting those with similar aspects in Canada. Students will work in groups of three, to identify the aspect of society they will study and a country that interests them and prepare to teach their class what they have learned. They will have three weeks to gather the information, organize their work, and develop a presentation for the class. They will be responsible for developing part of the class Web site, providing a handout for the class, creating visual materials for "teaching" their peers, and using one aspect of the arts for sharing information.

While the students are working on these projects, the classroom teachers plan to do a literature unit on stories from world cultures. Students will keep response journals, read independently a variety of literature, and create several pieces of writing. Mathematics class will include lessons on world monetary systems and currency exchange.

This brief overview immediately suggests that these two teachers will need many support materials to teach this unit, plus a plan to help organize group activities, skills to be taught, assessment procedures, and ways to celebrate and share student work. The unit requires heavy use of ICTs for student writing, information searching, and project presentations. The class Web site will also act as a repository for student work. If these two teachers work together, they can pool their efforts and work more efficiently. If they add the teacher-librarian to the team, then they gain much more than an "extra body": they have someone who can teach in some of the key areas outlined below.

Direct Teaching of Information Skills

In the World Cultures project, the teacher-librarian teaches skills such as note-taking, effective online searching, reading information texts, and many more. In the past, the teacher-librarian ran an isolated library program where these skills were taught out of sync with classroom programs. Now when classroom teachers are preparing to set up a research project for students, they may use the CPPT process and meet with the teacher-librarian to more effectively teach these skills. For example, if these two Grade 4 classes totaling 48 students were divided into groups of 16, then three groups could rotate through instructional sessions in the school library, where they would gain help with their research and presentation projects. The two classroom teachers could rotate the same groups through other tasks. This arrangement lowers the teacher-student ratio for instruction, provides chances for differentiated learning, and ensures that any resources available are accessible to all students.

Teaching Literacy Skills

In a similar way, when students are setting out on a writing project, a novel study, or other literacy-focused work, classroom teachers can call on the teacher-librarian to help plan and teach publishing workshops, booktalks, and Web site development projects. The Grade 4 students mentioned above will need support in creating their Web materials, finding the world literature they are to read, and accessing online literature sources. They will also need help creating visual materials for their presentations, as well as lessons in writing information texts.

Promoting Reading

Every teacher knows this is fundamental to good literacy teaching. All teachers encourage reading, model good reading habits, and when working together, they can create some amazing and exciting school-wide reading promotion projects (see Chapter 3 for specific ideas). No classroom teacher would have all the resources for a World Cultures literature study. The teacher-librarian could create displays, provide a readers' advisory to students selecting materials, and "feed" these classrooms special books, award-winning books, or new additions to the school library.

A Focus on the Ethical Uses of Information

This area demands more attention from teachers all the time. The World Wide Web (WWW) offers such easy access to information that many bad habits can emerge from students who do not understand and accept the principles of intellectual property rights, the ethical uses of information, as well as the implications of plagiarism. The teacher-librarian can act as the mediator here, emphasizing for students what the issues are and what their responsibilities entail. Exploring World Cultures would send students out onto the WWW to explore many information sources; it would provide the perfect opportunity to plan and teach lessons on the ethical uses of information. In addition, since the students are expected to "teach" what they find to their peers and create their own Web information, they would need to learn how to cite sources, create reference lists, quote texts, and request permission to use material. This awareness is particularly important when it comes to visual images, which many people seem to feel are there for the taking.

Developing Innovative Web Sites

Teacher-librarians often know a lot about and are comfortable with new information and communication technologies (ICTs). Also, the school library usually has the latest in ICT equipment, such as data projection systems, several computer workstations, scanners, printers, and multimedia packages. In the World Cultures project, the teacher-librarian could present an overview of effective Web design using examples from sites around the world. Classroom teachers and the teacher-librarian could work together to plan for the content and layout of a project Web site, establishing a meaningful role for students and creating the site. They could also get together to mount students' projects at the school homepage and set up school-to-school online learning projects.

Celebrating Student Learning

The school library is the perfect place to have students gather and present projects that their classroom teacher and the teacher-librarian collaboratively planned. They can launch their Web sites, open displays of their work, read their poetry, share their stories, or involve parents and the whole school in celebrating all they did on a recent novel study, research project, art activity, or other project. World Cultures lends itself well to bringing the small groups together to share their projects and represent one world community.

Planning the Use of Traditional and Digital Resources

The school library may be the source of many and varied resources, but it is useless for a classroom teacher to look for all the resources on World Cultures, for example, the day before the project is to begin. By using the CPPT process, classroom teachers and the teacher-librarian can plan for the use of the materials that will be required by many students; the teacher-librarian will have time to gather the materials and ensure their availability when needed.

A Collaborative Planning and Teaching Process—the CPPT

The planning time needed to develop projects or activities will vary depending on the nature of the activity. Types of planning sessions that may occur between the teacher-librarian and the classroom teacher are (1) formal meetings, (2) impromptu discussions, and (3) e-mail exchanges. Formal sessions are scheduled into the timetable or at regular times after school. Sometimes, the planning forms part of grade-level meetings, and sometimes, the sessions are called specifically to tackle an upcoming thematic unit or literacy project. Impromptu sessions tend to happen "on the run" when classroom teachers and teacher-librarians meet in the hallway, at recess, during a "prep" time, or even after school. Typically, these sessions are quick chances to see how the other person's part of the work is evolving, to share a resource, and to update each other. Finally, e-mail is a great way to connect quickly, send each other Web resources to check out, and share documents.

Depending on their styles, the planning partners may develop a planning guide and use it to track planning sessions, to keep lists of resources, and to outline the learning outcomes, suggested activities, and ideas for assessment. By following a planning guide, the teacher-librarian and classroom teacher will stay organized and focused, while recording what they have accomplished. (A blank model appears as an appendix on page 116.)

Inherent in the CPPT process is an understanding that each member of the planning team has specific tasks to complete, either before the next planning session or in time to begin the learning activity. For example, if a set of 10 learning stations is planned, each team member may organize five learning stations. Partners decide who will teach what part of the activities. They may decide to split the class in two, with the classroom teacher teaching a lesson to one half and the teacher-librarian helping the other half search several Web sites; then, they simply switch groups. They share the setting up of a schedule for the project. If the school library is structured with a flexible schedule, then the class of students may be able to come for four days in a row and complete the project over those four class periods. In some instances, one partner may assess one area of the project and the other assesses a different learning component. Suffice to say, just as the partners share in the planning, they share in the teaching, assessing, and celebrating.

Such a model for curriculum development and implementation allows for school-wide development of information literacy, ensuring that all students have a similar opportunity to achieve these skills. Some might argue, why do we really need the teacher-librarian? Can't the classroom teacher do this alone? Of course, if necessary, the classroom teacher can do this alone; however, when the teacher can work with a teacher-librarian, the work is more effective and efficient, and has the consistency that planning collaboratively provides. On the one hand, the classroom teacher has expertise in three areas: knowledge of students, knowledge of the core curriculum, and knowledge of classroom pedagogy. On the other hand, the teacher-librarian has expertise in these areas: knowledge of resources, knowledge of information and traditional literacies, and knowledge of resource-based learning. Learning increases exponentially when these combined areas of expertise are harnessed through collaborative planning and aimed at improving student achievement.

Stage 1: Setting Learning Outcomes

Usually, the teacher-librarian and teacher have at least one formal planning session at the beginning of the planning process. They set a time limit for the session, held in the classroom or in the school library. To plan their project or activity, they bring resources and ideas to the meeting, and use curriculum documents, information literacy outcomes, and library and classroom resources. The classroom teacher will likely have an initial idea of what specific outcomes she or he would like addressed and what content and skills students should learn. Together, the teacher and teacher-librarian set specific learning outcomes.

Stage 2: Designing Assessment Procedures

With a set of learning outcomes in place, the next task is for the partners to make decisions about assessment, understanding that they will both take part in the process. For example, if the team develops a rubric, each member might assess and then compare scores. Some examples of how students' work might be assessed include rubrics, teacher observations, checklists, individual and peer conferences, learning logs, response journals, and mini-tests. Also, when students assess their own work and the project as a whole, it helps the classroom teacher and teacher-librarian plan for future projects.

Stage 3: Developing Learning Activities

What activities will allow for students to achieve the learning outcomes that have been set? The possibilities are endless; however, students' learning needs must always be kept at the forefront. It is important, too, that these activities allow choices for students. In the planning meeting, the classroom teacher will provide knowledge of students' learning styles and capabilities, of the grade-specific curriculum, and of the desired structure of the project or activities. This structure could be direct instruction sessions by the teacher-librarian or the classroom teacher, online learning activities, learning stations, guest speakers, field trips, and traditional research and inquiry activities. The teacher-librarian suggests ways for the classroom teacher to go beyond the type of learning that usually happens in the classroom, offering unique resources, access to community and human resources, and structuring the teaching time so both partners have teaching roles.

A large portion of the planning process will involve producing these learning activities. Both the classroom teacher and the teacher-librarian share in this task, possibly producing learning stations, activity booklets, or Web-based activities. They then make decisions about the organization of the students' learning, the actual projects, and the sharing of teaching responsibilities.

Stage 4: Celebrating the Learning

Another important part of the CPPT process is for the classroom teacher and the teacher-librarian to plan for a celebration of student learning. After a project is completed, the learning should be shared and celebrated with students, teachers, administrators, and parents. One way of achieving this is through an Open House, where everyone is invited to view the student projects and hear about the exciting learning that took place in the school library. Parents and community members could be invited to concerts, public speaking events, student author readings, book publishing events, a launching of Web sites, and the myriad of culminating activities that help wrap up a unit of study, a special literacy project, or a unique ICT activity. A celebration can also be as simple as an in-class sharing or the building of a bulletin board.

Celebrating the learning has several benefits. Students see the importance in the work completed and are recognized for their efforts. Teachers witness students discussing what they have learned, which once again confirms all the skills and knowledge students have acquired during the project. Finally, including parents and the community in the celebration provides a great opportunity to promote the school library program and show the incredible amount of literacy learning that happens there.

Factors That Contribute to Success

A curriculum planning process such as the CPPT reflects a school's commitment to developing a collaborative learning environment; it also reflects a school-wide perspective on fostering information literacy and on promoting and encouraging literacy. It shows families and the wider community that the school values the use of diverse learning resources, involvement in problem-solving activities, teamwork, and the application of learning to "real world" contexts. It begins with an administrative vision reflecting these commitments and then relies on the willingness of teachers to open up their classrooms to the teacher-librarian. It also depends on the ability of the teacher-librarian to demonstrate to the whole school that a school library program benefits all children and helps all teachers develop more effective literacy programs.

Here are some factors that help classroom teachers and the teacher-librarian succeed with the CPPT model:

- *A flexible timetable.* A teacher-librarian needs an open timetable so that classes wanting to work on a special project can get the time to do it. If the teacher-librarian spends the whole time overseeing book exchanges or enabling "prep" periods, then there is no time for developing information literacy and for promoting and teaching reading through the CPPT model.
- *Adequate staffing.* A school library does best with a full-time teacher-librarian, a qualified teacher with the extra training and expertise in school librarianship to manage the library and become a full teaching partner with classroom teachers.
- *Administrative support.* No innovation will be introduced in a school without strong administrative support and leadership. The administrative team needs to fully understand and accept the role of the school library and the teacher-librarian in the development of children's literacy. They lead by example and set expectations for the teacher-librarian and classroom teachers to plan together. They facilitate that collaboration in ways that ensure its success.
- *An educational plan.* The school comes to understand the role that a school library plays in literacy achievement. The whole staff accepts that all students need help in developing lifelong learning skills and a desire to read throughout their life—no one teacher can do this alone. All classroom teachers, all specialist teachers, all members of the administrative team, plus the teacher-librarian work together to develop a cohesive and dynamic literacy program founded on solid skills instruction and high-powered efforts to promote and encourage reading.

How One Teacher-Librarian Made a Difference to Student Learning

In one jurisdiction, Grade 4 teachers are responsible for developing a thematic unit on bridges that incorporates literature studies, math, science, social studies, art, and health. One teacher wanted students to use more resources than what the classroom offered and hoped to extend student learning by working with the school's teacher-librarian. The partners held three formal meetings and six informal sessions. The teacher-librarian came to play an integral role in the success of the unit.

Basing Activities on Learning Outcomes

The classroom teacher explained exactly what literacy outcomes and core curriculum areas she needed to address, some preliminary ideas and structure for the project, and her students' learning needs. She stated that she had 19 students and liked the idea of having them work in groups on learning stations. The teacher-librarian and the classroom teacher decided that they would develop nine learning stations so that most of the students could work in pairs. They did a lot of brainstorming.

The classroom teacher had the final say in what ideas could and should be utilized as she provided the knowledge of her students' abilities, what curriculum needed to be taught, and what literacy outcomes and activities had already been addressed in her classroom. Together, the partners developed activity ideas for the learning stations, each focusing on a different core curriculum area, using a variety of learning resources, and addressing many different learning styles. They divided the work of preparing the stations about equally, offering each other feedback and determining specific teaching responsibilities.

The learning stations enabled the students to use different resources, develop a variety of information skills, and acquire content knowledge on bridges. The activities for each station are described below:

Learning Station Summary

Station #1: Safety on the Confederation Bridge (Health)

Students will read information on how the construction company tried to keep their workers safe while they were building the bridge. They will also read about how Strait Crossing keeps travelers safe on the bridge and helps to protect the environment. Students will answer questions about this information and label and color a diagram on safety.

Station #2: Science Experiment: Bridge Materials (Science)

Students will use various materials to conduct an experiment that demonstrates how steel can easily rust from salt, sand, and water. Students will see how steel that is protected may not rust as fast. They will use the scientific process and complete a sheet that states their hypothesis, materials used, steps of the experiment, and the experiment's conclusion.

Station #3: Research Station (Language Arts, Information Literacy)

Students will use three different non-fiction books to answer questions about six types of bridges. They will use the index and table of contents of these books to obtain their information. They will have to decide which information best answers the questions. They will also draw sketches of the six types of bridges.

Station #4: Information Technology (Technology and Social Studies)

Students will use one Web site to interactively choose what type of bridge would be built in a certain location in a community. Students will use another Web site to learn information about a specific bridge, the Hartland. Students will read and answer questions about this Canadian bridge.

Station #5: Math

Students will use a blueprint drawing of a bridge to figure out bridge measurements. They will measure this blueprint in millimetres and then convert this measurement to metres for an actual measurement. In this station, students will also answer some bridge-related problem-solving questions that utilize their math skills.

Station #6: Viewing a Video (Language Arts)

Students will view a video, *Big Cable Bridges,* and then answer questions about the video. The video is about 35 minutes long and gives information on how bridges are built.

Station #7: Building a Bridge (Art)

Students will use any materials they like to construct their own small-scale bridges. They will have ideas from what they have previously learned about bridges.

Station #8: Skills (Language Arts)

Students will use a dictionary to look up and record meanings of words related to bridges. They will use four of these words in a sentence of their own. They will correct a paragraph that contains mistakes in capitals, spelling, commas, apostrophes, and periods. They will also have to find nouns and verbs in this paragraph.

Station #9: The Confederation Bridge (Social Studies and Language Arts)

Students will read information about how the Confederation Bridge between Prince Edward Island and New Brunswick came to be. They will learn about the plebiscite of 1988 where Islanders voted whether or not they wanted the bridge to be built. Students will then decide how they would have voted had they been there in 1988 and write three reasons for their vote. They will also read a picture book about building the bridge. After reading this book, full of interesting vocabulary, students will write a cinquain poem using words from the story.

Assessing the Learning

The classroom teacher wanted to develop an assessment rubric that focused on skills linked with the learning outcomes addressed. The partners had a formal meeting to discuss and construct the assessment tool.

The partners referred back to all the learning outcomes they had already identified in their planning guide. They knew that they would also be assessing the students through observation of their project work and the completed product itself. They wrote a rough draft of an assessment rubric that contained the following skills: information skills for reading, comprehending and answering questions, grammar and punctuation, problem solving, technology and viewing skills.

At a second formal meeting on assessment, the classroom teacher and the teacher-librarian finalized rubric details. They decided to teach students about this rubric and use it during their work on the learning stations for this project. The classroom teacher and teacher-librarian felt it was important for students to take part in their own assessment and to understand exactly how their teachers were evaluating them.

Here is a copy of the rubric that the teacher and the teacher-librarian developed.

Bridges Project Assessment Rubric

Student Name: _____ Date: _____

Using information skills to read, comprehend, and answer questions:

4	Strong	Student's answer contains all of the expected points.
3	Good	Student's answer contains most of the expected points.
2	Adequate	Student's answer contains some of the points. The student may be able to provide a more complete answer, but only with guidance or prompts.
1	Poor	Student's answer contains very few or none of the expected points. Even with guidance or prompting, the student demonstrates difficulty in completing the questions.

Comments:

Grammar and Punctuation:

4	Strong	Student's answer contains all capitals, periods, commas, and apostrophes where appropriate.
3	Good	Student's answer contains most of the capitals, periods, commas, and apostrophes where appropriate.
2	Adequate	Student's answer contains some of the capitals, periods, commas, and apostrophes where appropriate. With prompting or guidance, the student may be able to use the appropriate grammar and punctuation in his or her answers.
1	Poor	Student's answer contains very few or none of the capitals, periods, commas, and apostrophes needed. Even with guidance or prompting, the student demonstrates difficulty in using appropriate grammar and punctuation in his or her answers.

Comments:

Problem Solving:

4	Strong	Without guidance, the student was able to follow directions and create strategies to solve problems.
3	Good	With some guidance, the student was able to follow directions and create strategies to solve problems.
2	Adequate	With constant guidance, the student was able to follow directions and create strategies to solve problems.
1	Poor	The student experienced extreme difficulty, showed no understanding of concepts, and was unable to complete the problems.

Comments:

Technology Skills:

4	Strong	The student demonstrated a proficient use of technologies by using Web sites and retrieving information.
3	Good	With little guidance, the student demonstrated a good use of technologies by using Web sites and retrieving information.
2	Adequate	With constant guidance, the student demonstrated adequate use of technologies by using Web sites and retrieving information.
1	Poor	Only with constant guidance did the student complete questions using Web sites to retrieve information.

Comments:

Viewing Skills:

4	Strong	After viewing a video or DVD, the student's answers to questions contained all of the expected points.
3	Good	After viewing a video or DVD, the student's answers to questions contained most of the expected points.
2	Adequate	After viewing a video or DVD, the student's answers to questions contained some of the points. The student may be able to provide a more complete answer, but only with guidance or prompts.
1	Poor	After viewing a video or DVD, the student's answer to questions contained few or none of the expected points. Even with guidance or prompting, the student demonstrates difficulty in completing the questions.

Comments:

Implementing the Project

The teacher-librarian and teacher spent 12 days to implement and teach this project. The students came down to the school library/computer lab every second day for about an hour for about five weeks. There, they applied their content knowledge and developed skills in problem solving, information literacy, reading, writing, and technology. As planned earlier, they were organized into eight groups of two and one group of three and rotated to a different station each day. Since the learning stations involved using a variety of resources, some groups of students worked in different rooms. For example, the station that required viewing a video was located in an adjacent empty classroom and the art station was located in the art room that was located right across the hall from the library/computer lab. It was fortunate to have the computer lab in the same room as the school library, a definite asset for easy integration of technology into this library project.

Any direct teaching of theme content was completed prior to the students working on the learning stations, seen as opportunities for students to apply newly acquired skills and knowledge. Both the teacher-librarian and the classroom teacher facilitated student work in the learning stations by circulating and helping students work in their groups.

In each session, the partners used the assessment rubric to monitor student work and provide support for further teaching. They also shared the rubric with the students who used it to know exactly what was expected of them during the project. The classroom teacher took notes of any observations made of her students' learning and discussed the assessment of the students with the teacher-librarian.

Reflecting Collaboratively

The teacher-librarian and the classroom teacher also took time to reflect on how well the learning stations served their purposes. It is impossible to produce perfect learning stations the first time that they are implemented; this collaborative reflection produced insights into how these stations could be revised and enhanced for future use.

Celebrating the Learning

In this instance, the Grade 4 students came to the school library with their projects and set up a display for the whole school. All classes visited the school library to see the work of the students who "taught" and explained to the other students what they had learned throughout this library project.

Benefits of Partnership for Student Learning

As the teacher and the teacher-librarian reflected on their success with the Bridges theme, they developed a list of key benefits from using the CPPT process. In summary:

- CPPT helps organize planning.
- CPPT ensures student learning.

- CPPT benefits the collaborators.
- CPPT focuses educators on assessment.
- CPPT works in other contexts.

Comments from the contributors are incorporated into the text that follows.

- *CPPT helps organize planning.* Both partners felt that they were better curriculum developers when they sat down and planned together. "You are thinking of all the parts of the process; you don't leave out anything. The process offers better organization for the planning discussions. You are there in the beginning, you see it developing, you are going through the process . . . and then you see the outcomes and the evaluation. You have the whole picture."

- *CPPT ensures student learning.* When the teacher-librarian is added to the teaching process, there is someone else to work with students, keep them focused, and provide help as needed. These teachers found that they could "cover more ground" and work with the outcomes in a rich, meaningful way.

> There is no down time, no delay in learning. That is one thing I noticed about this whole thing—the kids are all purposeful all the time. In this model, the students aren't sitting waiting for help. They get help right away and keep on working. I think this model is fantastic.
>
> We covered all the areas of the curriculum and a lot of outcomes. We made it more interesting by having all the different stations. By having the curriculum integrated, it added to the interest level. I found the students looked forward to the changes in the stations each day, the variety of them. Students need variety and it wasn't like work to them. I never had one complaint.
>
> With more teachers planning learning in different ways, we create learning stations that address all the children's learning styles. Eventually, all the children's strengths are met and they enjoy it more.

> One student commented, "It was fun and we got to do different things, build a bridge, do an experiment, go on the computer, and watch a video where I learned some things about bridges."

- *CPPT benefits the collaborators.* A collaborative team that has developed trust, mutual respect, and open communication with each other provides many opportunities for teacher feedback and support. The classroom teacher especially acknowledged the benefits of working together. "In a small school where there is only one teacher for the grade, you tend to feel isolated. This way you get another teacher's support . . . If you sensed you were going in the wrong direction, someone was there to help provide you with clarification."

  Another benefit for the collaborators was how the process provided an environment for sharing ideas: "I found it was a great learning experience for me, the whole process of working with the people involved." Such comments reflect the philosophy of the CPPT process which recognizes that the collaborative sharing of ideas and knowledge creates opportunities to learn from others, construct new knowledge, and build positive working relationships.

- *CPPT focuses educators on assessment.* The benefits of the CPPT process spread to these educators' assessment of students' learning. By following this guide, the team's planning meetings ensured early discussions of how the projects would be assessed and evaluated. "When we discussed assessment at the beginning of the projects, our discussions were more focused on the entire process. We were then able to develop opportunities for assessment that better reflected the curriculum outcomes and the student learning that we wanted to address. Using the CPPT guide proved to be a helpful tool in these discussions." The classroom teacher noted, "We talked about evaluation together and this gave everyone ownership and responsibility."

- *CPPT works in other contexts.* Through collaboration and a sharing of ideas, participants come to execute a collective vision, goals, and outcomes all aimed at student achievement. This suggests that when key elements of the CPPT process are present, it could be successfully used in other contexts. For example, a school ICT teacher could use this model with classroom teachers when planning technology outcomes and activities for students' learning in the computer lab.

As the partnership experience above exemplifies, when the relationship between the teacher-librarian and classroom teachers is based on mutual respect and a willingness to acknowledge each others' ideas, student learning flourishes and literacy programs improve.

3

Teacher-Librarians and Classroom Teachers: Partners in Promoting Reading

Ray Doiron

The teacher-librarian and the classroom teacher can form a powerful partnership for promoting and developing reading. Working together, they can bring children and books together through read-alouds, booktalks, author studies, genre studies, silent reading, book buddies, book festivals, and celebrations. All teachers will agree that turning children on to reading and fostering lifelong reading is a major goal. From the moment students begin school, teachers try many "tricks of the trade" to get them reading.

Today's literacy programs are built on the principles of direct instruction in the skills and strategies needed to read successfully, plus numerous activities to motivate students to read. Classroom teachers recognize that they need to do more than simply teach literacy skills; they must develop a stimulating program that will encourage their students to read.

At the same time, teacher-librarians develop rich collections of books and other resources which support the classroom teachers' instructional program and provide students with a wealth of choices for personal reading. They select books at different reading levels and on almost every topic imaginable, and from these, students choose books for independent reading in the classroom and at home. Teacher-librarians know that they need to do more than simply buy books and put them on the shelves; they must develop comprehensive programs that get books into the hands of their students and encourage them to read every chance they get.

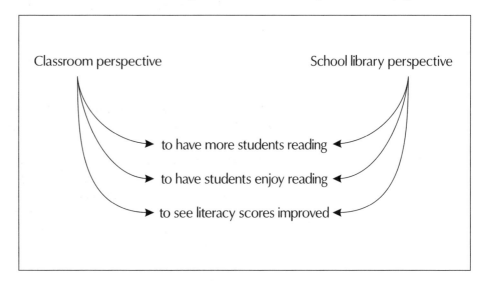

Classroom perspective   School library perspective

→ to have more students reading ←

→ to have students enjoy reading ←

→ to see literacy scores improved ←

This chapter explores what can happen when classroom teachers and teacher-librarians combine their efforts to increase and improve students' reading. When these educators work together, they can take a school-wide literacy initiative which promotes the use of a broad range of reading materials, encourages and motivates students to read, and establishes the school as a reading community.

The Quantity and Quality of School Library Resources

Classroom teachers need access to a wide range of resources to foster literacy, while students benefit from a wide range of books to choose from as they explore their reading interests and come to read more and more. Research by Keith Curry Lance confirms that schools whose libraries have well-developed instructional programs and well-stocked resource collections contribute to higher student achievement. In these schools, the school library is a focal point for learning and a centre for literacy promotion and development.

Stephen Krashen, in a 1998 article in *Educational Leadership,* also makes a strong connection between the number of books per student in the library and students' scores on tests of reading achievement. Students need many opportunities to practise their emerging literacy skills, so access to a wide collection of resources is essential to their developing the lifelong reading habit. Increasing the size of the school library collection has also been linked to higher levels of independent reading, increased use of the school library, and overall positive attitudes towards reading. Not only is the size of the collection important, the quality of items chosen for the school library must be high as well.

This collection needs to be selected by someone who knows the curriculum, as well as the reading interests of the students. The expertise of the teacher-librarian ensures that budget dollars are spent wisely to meet both of these criteria. The teacher-librarian knows the latest award-winning books and stays abreast of publications that will help with common curriculum topics, such as protecting the environment and exploring space. The teacher-librarian reads book reviews, examines Web sites for appropriateness, and develops a balanced collection of resources which reflect current information, popular and award-winning authors, and a variety of formats.

How Teacher-Librarians Help Classroom Teachers Promote Literacy

With the establishment of a strong school collection comes the responsibility to get resources from that collection into the hands of students and teachers for learning and teaching. Through a wide variety of cooperatively planned activities, teacher-librarians can exert a powerful influence in developing a school-wide focus on literacy. In most cases, they simply broaden the context for traditional promotional activities so that the school library plays a more significant role.

There are six major ways teacher-librarians can work with students and teachers to promote literacy:

- sharing the excitement of reading
- showing how resources promote students' diverse cultures
- making links to the wider community
- leading school-wide reading incentive programs
- developing other literacies, including visual and media literacies
- working in traditional literacy activities, to help students with writing projects, reading comprehension, and information skills

Sharing the Excitement of Reading

The teacher-librarian shows enthusiasm about reading and knows about the best books for encouraging children to read. At every opportunity, the teacher-librarian highlights new books, talks to teachers about the latest award-winning books, suggests sequels and follow-up books to ones recently read in class, and acts as the school's "town crier" for books and reading. When new books arrive, the teacher-librarian may make morning announcements about them and build displays to attract attention to them.

The teacher-librarian may also seek out other audiences. For example, he or she might organize a teachers' book club where new books and authors are discussed and celebrated, or make presentations to encourage and inform parents about reading with their children. The teacher-librarian often sends teachers and administrators current professional articles that match their interests, perhaps identified during staffroom conversations, staff meetings, or professional development sessions. Doing this saves colleagues time in locating the latest of research and information on literacy.

In the instructional context, the teacher-librarian models reading with every project and learning activity planned for the students.

Reading aloud is a key example of how that modeling has a major impact on student motivation to read. Immediately after the read-aloud, a student will likely want to borrow that book and other students will want to take home books suggested by the teacher-librarian for their independent reading.

Tips on Reading Aloud

If you haven't read the book already, read it to get a sense of its content before you start reading aloud.

Choose books that excite you or that excite your students. It is hard to read a book you don't enjoy, especially if it's long.

Be sure to set the context, mood, and purpose of the book.

Read with expression. A monotone is hard to listen to. Vary your pace, too. Slow down to build up suspense; speed up during exciting scenes.

Create voices for difference characters if you enjoy it, but doing so is unnecessary for a good reading. As long as you read with expression and enthusiasm, a story can be read effectively in a straightforward manner.

Read at a moderate pace, not too fast. Listening is a challenge for many children, and you don't want to leave them behind. Picture books require time for enjoying the illustrations.

Feel free to stop and discuss the book if you and your listeners want to. Answer questions as they come up. Be sure to adjust your discussions to keep large-group sessions well paced. How much you want to stop and explain new words is up to you. If they can be understood in context, you may want to keep reading. Stopping often to explain can undermine the story's impact.

Keep in mind that children can look bored or restless and still be listening. Some children need to be moving around or fidgeting with something. The real question is, are they following the story? If so, let them squirm or even draw pictures as they listen.

Sometimes, a book will lead to conversations afterward, sometimes not. Play it by ear. Either way is fine.

Include plenty of information books in your read-aloud program. Students love to learn about the world. They will enjoy your sharing of ideas and information.

If your students are not enjoying the book, do not finish it. You don't want to abandon a book quickly, but if a book has not sparked interest after several sessions, try another one. If this is a pattern, you may want to switch to shorter books and build up to longer ones.

Try reading a few poems together at a time. Start with limericks, nonsense rhymes, and other heavily rhythmic poems—be brave and try a rap—and you will be surprised how much fun you and your students have with poems.

For variety, you might read an article, letter, a press release or an excerpt from a diary or logbook.

The teacher-librarian can prepare booktalks that arouse interest in particular books or authors without giving too much away. Students love to be tantalized about a subject, topic, genre, favorite hero, and any exciting addition to the school library collection. Booktalks are also an excellent way to provide students with information about available titles or text sets for independent reading or literature circles. Sometimes, classroom teachers ask the teacher-librarian to prepare a series of booktalks, to be given in the classroom or in the school library; these talks can help launch an author study, a new theme, or a special project. Alternatively, classroom teachers may do this. Students enjoy booktalks and quickly make choices based on what they hear.

Nancy Keane's Booktalks—Quick and Simple This site offers many examples of booktalks for teachers and teacher-librarians written by professionals and students alike. There are reading lists, tips on giving a good booktalk, and sample booktalks arranged by age and subject.

http://nancykeane.com/booktalks/

Once teachers have modeled the booktalk, it is easier for students to present their own booktalks. Booktalks allow them to practise oral reading and writing skills, share their opinions, and make recommendations. Teachers could use them as an assessment tool to evaluate students' understanding of genre and themes, and to encourage discussion about literature in the classroom and school library.

Giving Booktalks

Provide information, but not too much.

Give the title, author name, other titles, if part of a series, and genre.

Use a hook to entice the reader. For example, dress up like a character, bring in an object that relates to the book, or show a movie trailer, an online video clip, or a Web site with virtual tours.

Briefly describe what happens in the book or outline the key information found in it

If talking about a story, tell about the main characters and the setting.

With an information book, introduce the author as a scientist, historian, or writer.

Excite interest perhaps by showing key illustrations or photographs or sharing any funny parts of the book.

Don't reveal too much!

Read aloud.

Select one or two key passages that say something about the setting, time period, or main characters.

Read only short excerpts (maybe half a page).

Be sure to choose descriptive and exciting sections, weird facts, or humorous bits for the read-aloud.

Mention related titles.

Provide examples of similar books that the students may already know.

Identify other books that are good examples of this genre or theme.

Note other titles by this author.

Explain how this book is like others you have read.

Express your opinion.

Tell students what really excites you about this book.

Explain why you recommend the book (or not).

Leave students wanting more . . .

Classroom teachers and teacher-librarians can collaborate in the teaching of how books work by developing mini-lessons on book parts, such as table of contents, index, and glossary, or by reading a chapter and discussing how well the title matches chapter content. It is important to teach students how books are organized, sequenced, and presented. They need to know fiction from information books, the characteristics of a particular genre, how to read information text, and how to use this information to write. This "talk about books" is crucial not only in emergent reading, but as reading fluency is developed and new reading challenges are presented to students. Often, the teacher-librarian is able to incorporate much of this teaching in activities held in library classes and planned collaboratively with the classroom teacher's program in mind.

The teacher-librarian also models for students the need to broaden their reading choices and genres, such as fiction, information books, and magazines. Balancing reading choices to include picture books, novels, information books, magazines, and other texts helps students strengthen their reading skills and text comprehension: it furthers their ability to master all sorts of subject areas later in school life and helps them function in the wide variety of contexts they encounter throughout life.

At book exchange times, when students come into the school library to choose new books for independent reading, the teacher-librarian can help guide student choices. It is crucial that students have access to some sort of "readers' advisory service" in the school library to help them nurture new interests while feeding their old favorites. Some children have keen interests in particular subject areas, such as space, friends, and animals. If a student wants books on whales and seems to look for the same topic every time, that student may quickly exhaust the supply of available books. It makes sense to point out magazines on whales, information books on individual whales and the family of whales, biographies of scientists who study whales, novels and stories about whales, and information books on other sea mammals. It is also worthwhile to recommend Web sites that have more information, games, or images of whales. The idea here is to take a strong interest and help the student develop a habit of balancing reading.

The teacher-librarian can help students broaden their reading interests beyond the formula text that many keep reading. Suggesting alternatives, sequels, latest popular titles, and peer-recommended books can really help students increase the variety in their reading choices.

Be sure to visit **Read∗Write∗Think**, a Web site with a full range of literacy lessons and literacy activities that help teach and promote various aspects of literacy.

http://www.readwritethink.org

Showing How Resources Promote Students' Diverse Cultures

Our world is shrinking in terms of the contacts, the visual images, and the shared cultural experiences we have every day. The resources we use for literacy instruction, whether from the classroom or the school library, must reflect our multicultural world. We recognize and celebrate the rich cultural heritage and valuable contributions made by our Aboriginal peoples as well as all who come to Canada. Since we strive to be a society based on equity and freedom for all, our students require a rich and diverse literacy program that will reinforce and strengthen these values.

Projects in which classrooms connect to classrooms around the world help teachers develop students' information and communication skills while reinforcing the values of diversity, equity, and freedom. Imagine students' excitement when they see they have e-mail from their friends in a school from another corner of the world or when they go online and share class projects with international classrooms.

The school library, with its diverse set of resources and engaging educational programming, is often the main source for many of these connections to other peoples. Here are some examples of how teachers engage students in meaningful cross-cultural activities:

- preparing an overview of the local community and mounting the information on the World Wide Web
- sending the community study electronically for another school to share and then several days later receiving a similar message from the other school
- establishing e-pals with students from other cultures and building dialogue journals with a writing partner in another country

These examples indicate how partnering projects allow students to get to know themselves better by sharing their identities with others. Such projects require planning and someone to make the initial contact or connection. Often, the teacher-librarian can take the lead here and help classroom teachers integrate such projects into their literacy programs, as well as content areas such as social studies and science.

Resources such as these can be a start for classroom teachers and teacher-librarians to collaborate and build projects that will promote the values of diversity, equity, and freedom in the global community.

The Global Classroom This site is organized around all levels of the curriculum with many simple project ideas from Times Around the World, Authors in Residence, and The Art Room. There are hints on starting projects and making contacts internationally.

http://www.globalclassroom.org/

The Global Education Network This portal offers information and project ideas in five areas: peace and justice, environment, human rights, development, and alternative media. There are also dozens of links and several curriculum units available.

http://www.global-ed.org/english/

The EarthWatch Global Classroom A comprehensive site, it has many links to researchers and scientists who take students on virtual tours and provide lessons online for the classroom. "Virtual Expeditions" and "Teachers Teaching from the Field" offer rich authentic learning experiences.

http://www.earthwatch.org/ed/olr/resources.html

Teacher-librarians help teachers and students access cultural materials of people in their local communities and from cultures around the world. Whether it is a major social studies unit on Aboriginal peoples, a celebration of immigrants, or a thematic unit exploring a group's customs and beliefs, the school library is a valuable source of materials: these will encourage students to learn more about their own culture and others. The teacher-librarian may set up *displays* that highlight the festivals and celebrations of different cultures or host a *storytelling festival*, where teachers or guest speakers share stories from the folklore of diverse groups and help raise awareness and respect for those people who appear different—hearing the stories of others reminds students that people understand the world differently and enables teachers to help children see connections in their culture. Children learn about themselves and others through the literature and information materials found in the school library.

Making Links to the Wider Community

In schools where teacher-librarians and classroom teachers collaborate to promote literacy, the school library is seen as a gateway to the world of resources beyond the school's walls. It is, first and foremost, a shared, physical, on-site collection of learning resources used by all teachers and students; in addition, it provides access to local human/community resources, resources from other libraries, and links to online databases, virtual tours, and various Web resources. Although classroom teachers try to develop classroom libraries, these never have the full range of resources offered by a school library. The teacher-librarian collects books and materials that support the classroom program, perhaps setting them up on a temporary basis in the classroom or as an information station in the school library for students to take and use in classroom projects.

The teacher-librarian often acts as a community contact setting up guest speakers or experts in curriculum projects, arranging field trips to local facilities, and locating useful community resources not normally housed in the school library. For instance, in a thematic unit, Animals in Our Community, the teacher-librarian arranged for a guest speaker on local mammals to provide expert information for students and set up a field trip to a pond, which allowed students to study and draw local habitats and animals. All such activities and their related resources excite children about learning, while encouraging them to read widely.

Leading School-wide Reading Incentive Programs

Classroom teachers and teacher-librarians can have a great deal of fun in their efforts to promote reading. Reading incentive programs involve students and teachers in fun activities that challenge students to read. Here are some examples.

- One class could challenge students in the next class to see who could read the most books. The teacher-librarian could select several titles and have children read and vote for their favorites.
- A school could run a One Book, One School program where a book is chosen and as many people as possible read the book at the same time and then discuss and share their reactions. One class or one grade could run a similar project.
- School-wide reading festivals celebrate reading. Each class could select a favorite book and set up a display about that book in the school library or somewhere else in the school.
- Many school libraries set up summer reading programs, where students pledge to read so many books over the summer vacation, track each book read on pledge sheets, and pass in their completed forms for a small recognition in the new school year.

A search on the Internet for "reading incentive programs" would likely yield dozens of examples of successful school-wide programs.

School-wide reading incentive programs involve the whole school in increasing how much students read while promoting reading in each classroom. Students love these school-wide events which build tremendous school spirit among students, teachers, and the community. The best thing to do is to form a school committee and set a school goal that all children are encouraged to support; then, individual classrooms take the idea and work on it. For example, one elementary school set the goal that the students would read for one million minutes and the media attended when they reached it.

Developing Other Literacies

Classroom teachers today do more than develop reading and writing skills in students; they use literacy in a wide variety of learning contexts which require students to apply their reading and writing skills in varied ways. In a similar sense, the teacher-librarian focuses on more than developing information literacy with students; within the school library program, students are supported as they develop many literacies.

Visual literacy, the ability to understand and produce visual messages, is rooted in the idea that visual images are a language. Here, students are taught how to look at images and determine what messages the artist or photographer is trying to share. They can look at art prints, book illustrations, and online graphic images to develop their aesthetic appreciation and their understanding of the visual world. Showing students a powerful visual image can motivate them to read more. The popularity of I Spy books and the Eyewitness series attests to students' interest in highly visual materials. Many students, as well, enjoy looking at diagrams, charts, and drawings that present information in meaningful ways.

Media literacy is the ability to understand how mass media work, how they produce meanings, how they are organized, and how to use them wisely. More than ever, students need to have both sharp visual literacy skills and a well-developed media savvy.

Both media and visual literacy are rooted in **critical literacy**, which calls upon learners to examine images and media products with an eye for who wrote the message, what is the "real" message, and how is this image or media product trying to manipulate them. One way to do this is to ask students to list all the commercials shown during a favorite TV program. The next day, take the lists and categorize the advertised products and services. Who are they aimed at? What promises do they make? What ideas impressed students? How was humor used to convince?

Traditionally, with access to audio-visual materials such as filmstrips, 35 mm films, and television, teacher-librarians have been a resource for developing media and visual literacies. With the explosion of information through the Internet, they have an even bigger role in teaching students how to use and make media critically. Most research projects require students to access Web sites and to be able to sort credible sources from less authoritative ones. For example, learning the difference between an ".org" site and a ".com" site helps students see that information is presented for a variety of purposes. Checking the Web page to see when it was last updated is also a simple example of a habit students need to develop, to make critical use of Internet resources.

> **The Media Awareness Network** This comprehensive site offers media and visual literacy articles, activities, and lessons that are matched to learning standards and which focus on media as students see and use it. A great source for classroom teachers and teacher-librarians to build a collaborative unit on media in the lives of today's youth.
>
> **http://www.media-awareness.ca/english/index.cfm**

The new literacies of information and communication technologies (ICT), such as word processors, Web editors, presentation software, World Wide Web, and e-mail, are a major focus in both classroom and school library programs. As information and technology have increasingly shaped our society, the skills needed to function successfully have gone beyond basic reading and writing to include the skills and thinking associated with the use of ICT.

> Be sure to visit **The Literacy Web**, which has a full range of current literacy research plus many literacy activities that help teach all aspects of literacy.
>
> **http://www.literacy.uconn.edu**

These other literacies are also powerful forces for motivating reading and encouraging students to read widely and for various purposes. Today's media are at the heart of culture for young people—they are their way of interacting with their world. As educators, we need to be aware of the lure that technology has for students, while capitalizing on how new media, the World Wide Web, text-messaging, and other technologies can encourage students to read widely and frequently. We must be careful not to define reading just in terms of reading a novel and recognize that youth today read in many more contexts than their peers of years gone by.

Teachers and teacher-librarians can easily go beyond having their students use the Internet only for research projects. For example, one way to launch an author study in literature class is to take students to the author's Web site, where they will see a picture of the author, a list of titles, and often games and ideas. One Grade 5 teacher starts her day with a visit to Environment Canada's Web site, where the class views a satellite image of the weather systems over their area. The school library often has a dedicated computer, where students can use reference tools such as dictionaries and online encyclopedias; its presence encourages students to integrate these tools into their daily work.

Providing Diverse Traditional and Innovative Literacy Activities

Given the vast demands of today's curriculum with its comprehensive set of learning outcomes, plus the competition for students' interests and attention, classroom teachers and teacher-librarians need to work together to teach and promote literacy. Doing this effectively means looking for ways to enhance traditional best practices while incorporating new and innovative resources and methods. It will give a school's literacy program greater richness and potential for influencing and motivating young readers.

The combined efforts of classroom teachers and teacher-librarians will show students that reading happens in many contexts and will provide them with a variety of literacy models. Here are a few ways to accomplish this.

Encouraging Use of Information Books

In addition to the focus on in-class and in-library reading initiatives, there are plenty of other opportunities to integrate information books into common teaching methods that literacy educators use.

For instance, *book buddies* is a common program where students from higher grades work with students in lower grades. Pairs of students share books and read aloud. They can readily explore each other's reading interests and come back with good information books to share at the next book buddy session. The teacher-librarian can coordinate the use of library resources for book buddies in search of materials for their next session.

Teachers and teacher-librarians can work together to develop *author studies* where students learn about the person behind the books they love to read. There are many excellent information book authors who could be examined and celebrated in the same way. Authors such as Gail Gibbons, Linda Granfield, and Russell Freedman have much to teach students about the research and hard work that goes into writing quality information books. Setting up a library display of books by the author, leaving these books on reserve for the use of students studying that author, plus helping students in their writing of a short author biography, are examples of how the teacher-librarian can provide support.

Book publishing is also a common writing experience where students take a story through the writing process and produce a book complete with their own illustrations, cover design, table of contents, and author biography. Teachers who have taken this activity into the writing of information books report that students become excited about writing when they write about the world around them, the natural world, the world that informs their personal interests (Stead, 2002). Students also enjoy adding graphics, visual representations, and unique book design techniques to their information books. It opens a whole new and exciting world for teachers who balance their writing programs with opportunities for students to produce such books.

Balancing Reading Choices

Classroom teachers know their students well in terms of the skills they have developed in literacy. The teacher-librarian knows the latest interests and reading trends of students and can help connect them to books and other reading materials of interest. When they work together, they help students explore their reading choices and broaden their reading interests. The chart below has several suggestions to help classroom teachers and teacher-librarians achieve this.

Ideas for Developing Children's Reading Choices

Get to know the students with simple surveys of interests.

Examine the computer records in the school library to identify frequently signed-out items. Examine choices that girls and boys are making and share the information with teachers. Find new materials to support the choices identified. List titles that might complement or extend what students are reading.

Take a class set of magazines into the classroom for a silent reading period.

Choose an information topic and set up a display highlighting books on that topic.

Have a book buddies program and encourage buddies to choose books of interest to their reading partners.

To help balance reading choices, read aloud information books; doing so will motivate students to take these books for their independent reading.

Draw attention to graphic novels and new formats for information books—these make interesting and alluring choices.

Help students develop their own criteria for making reading choices: track their reading choices and then have a class discussion on common trends in their choices. What makes a book appealing to them? Why do they reject some? How do their peers influence their choices?

Genre studies have always been part of literacy programs where teachers teach students using historical fiction, science fiction, or fantasy. Under the expanded definition of their role, teacher-librarians gather examples of the genre being studied, do booktalks on the titles, and teach lessons on the characteristics of the genre, leaving plenty of time for students to do independent reading in the classroom. Displays highlighting authors and book titles from the genre also help promote the reading of books from that genre. Teachers may do a novel study using a core genre book and students could study further examples of the genre while in literature circles.

Holding a Poetry Festival

The teacher-librarian plans with the teachers which area of poetry each class in the school will study. Resources are collected and shared, and students spend several weeks reading and writing poetry. Everyone focuses on one week when the school holds its poetry festival. The poetry studies and the poems written by students are shared and celebrated in various events held in the school library—the school could hold similar festivals to highlight favorite authors or illustrators or feature storytelling or puppetry.

Exploring the World of Book Illustration

Literacy programs often focus on author studies as one way to raise awareness and understanding of being an author. Focusing on illustration would help a school learn about the many book illustrators who help bring stories alive for readers. As with the poetry festival, the teacher-librarian could coordinate the event by having each classroom choose a different illustrator, collect all their books, study their techniques, try using those techniques in art projects, and then celebrate the projects with an art exhibit set up in the school library and in the halls of the school. Parents especially will enjoy touring this art gallery of student work inspired by the work of professional book illustrators.

A School-wide Culture of Reading

For ongoing professional reading on literacy and school libraries, read "Literacy Links," featured in every issue of *Teacher Librarian: The Journal for School Library Professionals.*

As classroom teachers instruct students in literacy and promote it, the teacher-librarian reinforces traditional and critical literacy skills, teaches information, media, visual, and new literacies, and promotes lifelong reading. Providing children with access to a wide variety of reading materials is recognized as a crucial factor in literacy achievement, and classroom teachers need to work closely with the teacher-librarian to get students into the school library as often as possible. Using the school library as an extended classroom allows students to explore the widest variety of resources while using those resources for meaningful learning and independent reading. Schools need to create a culture for literacy that is nurtured and developed in the classroom, but expressed and fully realized throughout all aspects of students' learning. When classroom teachers and teacher-librarians work together, their efforts have greater impact and students learn that the whole school is a learning environment rich in the culture of reading.

4

Working for Social Justice in the School Library: Exploring Diversity, Culture, and Social Issues with Children's Literature

Lyndsay Moffatt

Dear Teacher,

I am a survivor of a concentration camp. My eyes saw what no man should witness. Gas chambers built by learned engineers. Infants killed by trained nurses. Women and babies shot and burned by high school and college graduates. So I am suspicious of education. My request is: Help your students become human. Your efforts must never produce learned monsters, skilled psychopaths, educated Eichmanns. Reading, writing and arithmetic are important only if they serve to make our children more human.

Author Unknown*

In a powerful way, this letter points to the important role of teachers and teacher-librarians in raising awareness of the social issues facing our youth today. School library policy at the international, national, and local levels identifies their responsibility for developing a collection of resources representing the diversity of the world out of school even if some of those materials are controversial, as well as "to provide support for the furtherance of social justice " (Clyde, 2005, p. 95).

During my experiences as a teacher-librarian in an inner-city school, I became convinced that the school library is a key site for raising issues about social justice. This chapter will outline some of the ways that a teacher-librarian can work with teachers to address issues of ablism, classism, heterosexism, racism, and sexism (see definitions). The chapter also features descriptions of resources that I have found useful in opening up discussions of equity issues with elementary-aged students. These tools enable teachers to get into these issues.

The School Library as a Natural Place for Social Justice Work

One reason why school libraries are a natural place to do social justice work with elementary students stems from the history of public and

---

* Cited in S. Berman's *Children's Social Consciousness and the Development of Social Responsibility*, page 11.

school libraries. Teacher-librarians may want to begin the school year with a short discussion about why we have public libraries and school libraries. Public libraries were first begun by working-class men who organized "reading rooms" so that regardless of disposable income, they could be informed about local issues and politics. School libraries were established for much the same reason: they are founded on the premise that all children should have access to print materials and information technology regardless of whether their parents can afford to buy them. In this way, the very existence of public libraries and school libraries is a testament to our society's commitment to social justice.

In addition, the school library is a natural place for social justice work as it is often the *only* place where the most marginalized students have access to print materials and information technology. Even if a community has a fantastic system of public libraries, the school library may be the only place where young children who want to read can gain access to reading materials for free. Many students visit the school library daily, but are unable to visit their local public library as their parents work and are not free to come with them. In this way, the school library becomes the only place that provides the youngest and poorest students with access to a wide range of reading material.

Why the School Library Should Be a Key Site for Social Justice Work

The school library, when adequately staffed and funded, is often the heart and soul of a school. All the students, staff, and parents are welcome in the library, typically the central meeting place in the school. When special guests come to the school, they are often given a tour of the library or asked to present their talks there. In many ways, the school library is like the family room of the school. As significant a physical space as the front foyer or the main office, it is a space in which the school presents to the community important aspects of its character. So, what goes on in the school library, what is on the walls and on the shelves, as well as what kind of technology it houses, all reflect the work and the values of the school. The impact of having materials that address social justice issues in the school library can be even greater than having such materials in a classroom collection: their presence means that the entire school community has made a place for these issues.

How the School Library Program Supports Social Justice Work

Teacher-librarians are well positioned to promote social justice work. They can have more flexibility in terms of content and instructional approaches. Also, when they support literacy in such ways as read-alouds or novel studies, or when they pilot social studies units or research projects, they usually have much control over their choice of materials. With the right resources, teacher-librarians can work with teachers to plan activities, such as storytelling, novel studies, and research projects, that will open up discussions about equity issues.

How to Make the School Library a Home for Social Justice

Teachers and teacher-librarians may collaborate to develop the school library as the school's centre for promoting social justice. When planning for this goal, there are three important aspects to consider: the library and school environment; the collection; and guest speakers or storytellers. Several prompts for reflection and assessment are outlined below.

The Environment

- Think about the kinds of posters and decorations that are on display. Do these artifacts reflect a wide range of abilities, cultures, genders, language groups, and socio-economic classes?
- Think about the books and other reading materials that are on display. Do they reflect a diverse range of abilities, cultures, genders, language groups, and socio-economic classes?
- Think about how teachers and the school library recognize Black history, Asian history, and women's history, for example. Are the contributions of people of color and women recognized throughout the year or only within designated months?
- Think about the kinds of holidays and events featured in displays. Are we creating displays for events such as Labour Day, Gay and Lesbian Pride Day, International Literacy Day (September 8) or the anniversary of the UN Universal Declaration of Human Rights (signed in 1948 and celebrated December 10 each year)?

The Library Collection

- Does the library collection reflect a diversity of abilities, cultures, genders, language groups, and socio-economic classes? Achieving this is particularly important if your school is situated within a multi-lingual, multi-cultural, mixed socio-economic environment, but is also important within a fairly homogeneous population. Often it is through literature that students learn to have empathy for people who seem different from themselves. Also, although students may live in a homogeneous population now, given the ever changing demography of global populations, chances are they won't when they grow up.
- Does the collection contain biographies of people who have worked for social justice, civil rights, or the environment? There are many titles on a number of activists and civil rights leaders written at a range of reading levels. For reluctant readers, simple biographies are often an early entry point into sustained reading.
- Are there dual language books or books in languages other than English? If your school serves a multi-lingual population, it is important to have a range of books that children can share with their families in their first language or that support English language learners.

Connecting with a parent from the target language community and asking for help shopping for the library is an effective way to involve parents and find suitable materials students will use.

Guest Speakers or Storytellers

- Do the people who come into the school as guest speakers or story-tellers reflect a diversity of abilities, cultures, genders, language groups, and socio-economic classes? People in the wider school community may be rich resources and may also assist teachers and teacher-librarians in identifying speakers who can address particular issues of social justice. There may also be a group of activist youths at a local high school who would be willing to visit and discuss their activities.

Resources to Help Begin Discussions about Social Justice Issues

Examples of Listservs
International School Library Association:
IASL-LINK
http://www.iasl-slo.org/ iasl-link.html#joining
Canadian Association for School Libraries:
CASL Listserv
http://www.caslibraries.ca/ people/support.aspx

An abundance of resources is available to help teachers and teacher-librarians engage in social justice work. An effective way to learn about what is available is to become acquainted with some of the smaller independent and specialty bookstores. For example, most large cities have women's bookstores or bookstores created to serve particular ethnic communities. These bookstores offer resources that will contribute to the creation of a library that reflects a diverse range of abilities, cultures, genders, language groups, and socio-economic classes. Teacher-librarian listservs may also be a useful resource towards this goal.

Exploring what is available online through an Internet search also helps teachers and teacher-librarians identify resources.

The resource lists that follow are designed to help teachers and teacher-librarians in elementary schools address issues of social justice, specifically, ablism, classism, heterosexism, racism, and sexism. They also include resources on how to work for peace.

Ablism

Ablism is discrimination against people who have mental or physical disabilities (Adams, Bell, & Griffin, 1997). When I explain it to my students, I say that ablism is being unfair to someone because they are unable to do something. Making fun of someone who can't run as fast as you can or teasing someone who needs glasses to help them see are examples. I also point out that it is ablist when buildings are designed without ramps for people who have trouble walking.

Thank You, Mr. Falker by Patricia Polacco
This story relates Polacco's own struggles with learning to read. It features a bully who torments her for being "dumb" and a teacher who likes all of his students equally. Polacco's beautiful illustrations capture the poignancy of her struggle.

My Friend Isabelle by Eliza Woloson
Charlie's mom tells him that "differences are what make the world so great." Simple text and beautiful illustrations help frame Charlie's celebration with Isabelle, a girl with Down's syndrome. As Charlie puts it, "Life is more fun with friends like Isabelle."

Susan Laughs by Jeanne Willis and Tony Ross
Susan laughs, sings, swings, dances, and swims through this book. Susan feels happy, sad, angry, proud, and shy. Susan is good and Susan is bad. Susan does and feels many things. It is not until the final page that the reader learns that Susan also uses a wheelchair.

Nathan's Wish by Laurie Lears
Nathan has cerebral palsy and can't get around without his wheelchair or walker. More than anything, he would like to find a way to help his neighbor, Miss Sandy, who cares for wounded birds. After meeting an owl with a broken wing, Nathan finds ways to help Miss Sandy and the birds.

Classism

Nice Work, Little Wolf by Hilda Offen
A poor young wolf is taken in by a family of pigs who treat him like a slave, running errands and building houses and swimming pools. At long last, Little Wolf rebels and the pigs flee, leaving him to invite his mother into the mansion proclaiming proudly "it's all my own work." The story is also a good resource for talking about ageism and sexism as the pig family is run on a hierarchy headed by the father.

In the Garden by Carolyn Mamchur and Meguido Zola
A Métis girl, given a packet of seeds when her grandmother dies, decides to plant a garden in the city where she is living—Winnipeg. Midway through the summer, her father goes on strike and she uses the vegetables from her garden to make soup for the hungry strikers.

Strike! by Maureen Bayless
Molly's mom is on strike at the local cannery. When Molly goes with her mom to the picket line one day, she learns that the line is understaffed because everyone has the flu. Mid-afternoon, word comes that a fleet of trucks will be trying to cross the line. With some quick thinking Molly uses her teddy bear and a note to cover the picket's weakest link.

Heterosexism

Who's in a Family? by Robert Skutch
This simple book reminds you that no matter what your family looks like, whether it is made up of a mom and a dad, a single parent, a grandma, two dads or two moms, children or no children—families are the people who love you.

King and King by Linda de Haan and Stern Nijland
The queen decides she wants the prince to get married and begins a hunt for the most suitable princess. What she doesn't realize is that the prince is far more interested in princes. In the end, both the queen and the prince are happy as the prince falls in love with a wonderful prince and they get married after all.

Classism is discrimination against people who are poor or working class. In simple terms, classism is being unfair to people who are poor or who have less money than you do because they are poor or have less money than you do. When I talk about this with my students, I often need to explain terms like *working class*, *middle class*, and *rich*. I also suggest that when employers treat people who are working for them badly, it is a form of classism because they are using their power over them. Teasing someone for being on social assistance is also classist.

Heterosexism is the belief that heterosexuality is the only natural, normal, acceptable sexual orientation. When I explain it to my students, I say it is being unfair to people who are gay or lesbian because they are gay or lesbian. But it is also heterosexist to make fun of children who have gay or lesbian parents. It is heterosexist to assume everyone is heterosexual and it is heterosexist to use the word "gay" or "lesbian" in a derogatory way. For example, if students say, "That's so gay," meaning the thing in question is not cool, their comment is heterosexist as it implies being gay is uncool.

Daddy's Roommate by Michael Willhoite
A young boy tells of his family which consists of his mom in one house and his father and his father's partner in another. As he explains it, "Gay is just another kind of love."

Heather Has Two Mommies by Leslea Newman
A story of a little girl who has lesbian moms, Mama Kate and Mama Jane. Although this book has been met by controversy, the story itself is far from challenging.

Asha's Moms by Rosamund Elwin and Michele Paulse
Asha's teacher doesn't believe she has two moms and Asha may be unable to go on the class field trip if she doesn't get her permission form signed "properly." Asha's moms and the principal help solve the problem.

Racism

Amazing Grace by Mary Hoffman
Grace loves to act out stories. At auditions for the school play one student tells her she can't be Peter Pan because she is Black. Another student tells her she can't be Peter Pan because she is a girl. Grace's Nana helps set things right and encourages Grace to be whoever she wants to be. One of the few books to directly address racism or sexism.

Bird Talk by Lenore Keshig-Tobias and Polly Keshig-Tobias
A young Ojibway girl comes home confused and sad after friends at school have been playing cowboys and Indians. Her mom and her sister comfort her and plan how she can address the game at the school. In Ojibway and English.

All the Colors of the Earth by Sheila Hamanaka
This poem celebrates the diversity of human skin colors and hair. The pattern-like text makes it useful for extension activities. One good idea is to have children illustrate the poem or write other verses.

Colors of Us by Karen Katz
When Lena and her mom take a walk through the neighbourhood, they find that all the different colors of friends and family remind them of treats, like chocolate, honey, peaches, cinnamon, and toffee.

This Land Is My Land by George Littlechild
Cree artist George Littlechild's paintings form a beautiful backdrop for his discussions about Aboriginal history and current challenges. This book, with its contemporary perspective, would be particularly useful for older students assigned research projects on Aboriginal peoples.

The Seven Fires: An Ojibway Prophecy by Sally Gaikesheyongai
This book discusses the Ojibway prophecy concerning the seven fires or seven eras of the Ojibway people. It would be useful for opening up discussions of the impact of European settlement on Aboriginal peoples.

Racism is discrimination against members of cultural, ethnic, or racial groups that have little social power by members of cultural, ethnic or racial groups who have relatively more social power. When I talk to students about racism, I say that it is being unfair to people who have a different color of skin than you do or speak a different language than you do.

Let's Talk About Race by Julius Lester
Newbery Honor Book author Julius Lester offers a compelling discussion of race. As Lester writes, race is part of the story of who you are, but it is only part of the story. Lester's gentle text reminds us that "beneath everyone's skin are the same hard bones."

Sexism

Beautiful Warrior by Emily McCully
Mingyi is destined to be married to a terrible brute unless she can best him in Kung fu. This challenge sends her to study Kung fu with a nun at the Shaolin temple. After a year of practice Mingyi defeats her opponent. Free to live her life as she pleases, she decides to follow the work of her teacher.

Ruby's Wish by Shirin Yim Bridges
Ruby, one of a hundred grandchildren living in a family compound in early 20th century China, wants nothing more than to study like her boy cousins and go to university. Her studies are set to end, though, when she reaches the age to marry. Ruby's fate seems decided until her grandfather hears her desire and writes to a local university to plead her case. Based on the life of the author's grandmother.

Pugdog by Andrea U'ren
Mike has a new puppy named Pugdog. Pugdog has a fine life of chasing squirrels and getting dirty until Mike discovers Pugdog is female. Mike then begins to dress Pugdog in silly uncomfortable outfits and tries to teach her to be ladylike. Pugdog grows miserable and then runs away. When Mike finds her again, he realizes his mistake and stops trying to make a lady out of her, telling her he loves her just the way she is.

William's Doll by Charlotte Zolotow
A classic tale of a boy who wants a doll so that he can learn how to care for it. William's brother and father don't understand, but William's grandma does and she makes sure that he gets the doll he longs for.

Piggybook by Anthony Browne
Mrs. Piggott is tired of cleaning up after her husband and sons so she runs away. In her absence the family learns how difficult it is to maintain a household. When Mrs. Piggott returns, her family begs her to stay and everyone begins to pitch in to do the daily chores.

Homelessness

Fly Away Home by Eve Bunting
A boy and his dad live at the airport. The matter-of-fact narrative told by the boy gives us a glimpse into their world as they cope with misfortune and homelessness.

Sexism is usually defined as the subordination of women by men. However, through my work in elementary schools, I feel this definition misses a lot of the ways in which boys and girls learn to reproduce sexism. In particular, the traditional definition ignores the kind of "gender policing" that young boys experience. When talking with students, I say that sexism is being unfair to someone because she or he is a girl or a boy: for example, saying someone can't play soccer because she is a girl, or saying someone shouldn't cry or play with dolls because he is a boy.

Working for Peace

The Big Book of Peace by Ann Durrell and Marilyn Sachs with illustrations by Maurice Sendak
This book features a range of material including fables, poems, biographies, and illustrations from well-known writers and illustrators. The stories about the roots of war are told on a scale that children can grasp. They include, for example, how envy between two girls escalates into a cold war and how a pair of princes squabble over their turf and eventually destroy each other's kingdoms.

Something Beautiful by Sharon Wyeth
A young Black girl learns the word "beautiful" in school and sets out to ask all of her neighbors what they think of as beautiful. A thoughtful meditation on finding beauty in the urban environment.

The Colour of Home by Mary Hoffman
A refugee boy from Somalia struggles with his new life in England until he begins to paint and talk to a case worker about his memories.

Sami and the Time of the Troubles by Florence Parry Heide and Judith Heide Gilliland
In an unnamed war-torn country in the Middle East, Sami spends most of his days indoors, but he has heard of a day when the children marched for peace. Someday soon, he thinks, the children will march again.

Rethinking Globalization, published by Rethinking Schools, a collective of activist teachers, contains numerous activities related to social justice. These activities are suitable for upper elementary students.

Peace Begins with You by Katherine Scholes
This book offers a thoughtful exploration of what peace means and how to work for peace within our own communities and families, and in the world. Younger children may need help with the vocabulary in this book; however, they will likely understand the concepts.

Make Someone Smile and 40 Ways to Be a Peaceful Person by Judy Lalli
Simple text and photographs outline actions we can all take to work for peace.

Students as Advocates of Social Justice

In her early exploration of issues of gender in Kindergarten, *Boys and Girls: Superheroes in the Doll Corner*, Vivian Paley writes of a boy named Teddy who begins a class storytelling with the words "Once there was a boy named Pretty." Paley goes on to tell us how Teddy's classmates laughed him down and how Teddy abandoned his story and never returned to it. Although Paley does not explore this image extensively, the image of a Kindergarten boy trying to tell a story about a boy named Pretty has been rooted in my mind ever since I first read her book. When I think about Teddy and his story, I wonder what story he was about to tell. Maybe he was going to tell us the story of boy who was worthy of praise or maybe his was the story of an unconventional boy.

There are many ways to understand the scenario that Paley offers the reader. We could read it as an example of how children are socialized into different language communities, as it appears that Teddy was being taught by his peers that "Pretty" was an inappropriate name for his protagonist. Perhaps in this community, like in many other English-speaking communities, "pretty" is a term reserved for girls and is rarely, if ever, used for boys. This moment could be read as one in Teddy's grammatical development as he seems to be trying to use an adjective as a noun, something he might not do a year hence. This scenario could also be read as a moment of policing gender boundaries, as the children's laughter was unkind and seems somehow connected to the fact that Teddy was a boy or that his protagonist was.

Perhaps the best reading of this scenario is that Teddy was trying to tell a *different* story. Regardless of what happened in that classroom and to Teddy and his story, it seemed Teddy was trying to open up a space in his classroom for a new kind of story, one in which boys were allowed to be pretty or gentle or anything they pleased.*

This reading of Teddy's story reminds us that our students are our allies in our struggles to create new social worlds. Time and again in my work as an elementary teacher-librarian, I have learned when given the opportunity to do so, children are highly capable of assessing and responding to issues of social injustice.

The more teachers and teacher-librarians work with students, the more they will realize that they do not need to re-socialize them in order to create a more equitable and just society. Most children come to school with a kind of innate sense of fairness and justice. The more we listen to children, the more we will recognize that if we want to create a just world, we need to create spaces for them to talk and for them to raise questions about how things are and how they could be.

We owe our students the chance to expand their gut-level and passionate ideas of fairness and justice. In listening to and watching our students, we will respond to our growing responsibility to provide support for them to critically address the many cruel and unjust notions of ability, race, class, gender, and language that persist in our society. If we choose not to engage students in discussions of social justice and actions to correct injustice, we leave them without the tools to transcend the limited perceptions and narrow opinions that still pervade our world.

---

* In this way, Teddy reminds me of the main character in the movie *Educating Rita*. Rita tires of all the roles foisted on her by friends and family, and in response to hearing yet another round of a popular song says, "There must be better songs to sing."

5

Building Young Children's Comprehension of Informational Text Structures during Daily Read-alouds

Margot Filipenko

One role that the teacher-librarian plays is that of the "information resource specialist" whose prime responsibility is to teach students how to manage information (Doiron, 1999). This role is crucial in the Information Age when the ability to understand, evaluate, and use informational texts is "central to success, and even survival, in advanced schooling, the workplace, and the community" (Duke, 2000, p. 202). Research by Pappas and Filipenko shows that, with support, even young children can enjoy and understand informational texts; however, to successfully introduce young children to informational texts requires collaboration between the teacher-librarian and the classroom teacher. Specifically, the teacher-librarian can support young children in their information literacy development in these ways:

- by developing a school library collection that includes not only storybooks and poetry, but also non-fiction that suits the interests and range of reading abilities of all children, including the very young
- by collaboratively planning and teaching with the classroom teacher—together they can address the skills and strategies students need to use information resources effectively

This chapter describes how the teacher and teacher-librarian can collaboratively support young children's knowledge and comprehension of informational texts through read-alouds. It focuses on the importance of identifying and designing developmentally appropriate activities for particular informational text structures. A unit on dinosaurs developed in an early childhood education classroom will illustrate how a teacher and teacher-librarian successfully introduced informational text structures to a class during read-alouds.

The Key to Understanding Informational Texts

Information texts are now recognized as a critical part of a comprehensive literacy program. In response, school library collections increasingly contain a variety of types of information materials, including books representing the unique text structures and features of informational texts. Richgels, McGee, and Slaton (1989) write that because the purpose of informational texts is to explain, describe, or inform, children must be able to detect how ideas are organized and related in what they read. Students generally have more difficulty reading informational texts than narrative texts, though. They have had less experience with them and these texts do not follow a set beginning-middle-end pattern; instead, how the information is organized depends on its type and purpose.

Text structure refers to the way in which the author has organized and developed ideas. In *Creating Literacy Instruction for All Children*, T. G. Gunning suggests that the key to understanding informational texts lies in the child's ability to comprehend these text structures. The most common text structures are as follows:

- *description* (Ideas are connected through description by listing important characteristics or attributes.)
- *sequence* (Facts, events, or concepts are arranged in sequence.)
- *cause and effect* (An effect is presented along with the cause or causes.)
- *comparison/contrast* (Similarities and differences among facts, people, events, or concepts are pointed out.)
- *question–answer* (A question is followed by an answer, sometimes in the form of a *problem* and *solution*.)

Writers often indicate which text structure organization they are using by providing clue words. These clue words provide information about the relationships between ideas. For example, clue words signaling the sequence text structure include *first*, *second*, and *next*. Clue words indicating the cause and effect text structure include *therefore*, *as a result*, and *because*. Clue words signaling comparison/contrast text structures include *like*, *different from*, and *however*. Clue words signaling question–answer structures include *how*, *what*, *when*, and *where*. Finally, clue words signaling problem and solution text structures include *problem*, *solution*, and *solve* (Richgels et al., 1989, p. 172).

Selecting Informational Texts

Language

Does the material

- use simple, straightforward vocabulary?
- include some specific scientific or technical terms?
- present special or technical terms in context?
- use short direct sentences?

Ideas and organization

Does the material

- present one idea at a time?
- provide specific and concrete information?
- show relationships among ideas that are explicit and simple (e.g., sequence, cause–effect, description)?
- use short paragraphs that begin with a clear topic sentence followed by details?
- use boldfaced titles and headings?

Graphics and Format

Does the material

- incorporate illustrations and graphics to support and provide content?
- show clear relationships between text and illustrations?
- have illustrations that elaborate and clarify the written text?
- use a readable type size, typically 14 point or larger?
- have small blocks of text with considerable white space?

Reading Information Books Aloud

As noted in Chapter 3, teacher-librarians have extensive training in and experience with promoting reading through read-alouds. It is important for them to read aloud to students, whether in Kindergarten or in Grade 12, and to provide excellent materials for classroom teachers to read aloud too. Although this chapter focuses on young children, teachers are wise to keep in mind that science teachers can read aloud articles related to study, and history teachers can read aloud primary sources, such as letters and diary entries. Benefits of reading aloud include the following:

- providing young children with a strong sense of what reading is all about
- helping young children develop a love of books
- developing children's listening comprehension
- encouraging children's understandings about the conventions of print and books
- helping young children learn that book language differs from everyday speech
- providing a bridge to a genre or text students may not choose or be able to read
- providing opportunities to point out concepts, facts, and how information is organized

Information Book Read-Aloud Strategies

Before the Reading

Set aside time for reading aloud daily.

Choose books on topics that are interesting and engage both you and the students.

Select text that enriches topic knowledge, vocabulary, experiences, and language.

Become familiar with text and text structures.

Activate prior knowledge by exploring what students may have experienced already on the topic.

Set a purpose for listening.

If this is a continuation of the same topic review what was read.

During the Reading

Read fluently and with expression.

Demonstrate comprehension strategies by thinking aloud.

Pause, if appropriate, to invite personal responses or predictions or offer clarification.

Observe the listeners' behaviors to check engagement and levels of enjoyment.

After the Reading

Involve students in discussion or retelling of the information.

Make the book available for students.

Extend the reading through the arts, writing, or additional reading.

Source: Based on http://www.manatee.k12.fl.us/curriculum/ Elements%20of%20Read%20Aloud.doc

A Sample Unit Based on Read-alouds

An early childhood teacher and teacher-librarian collaboratively introduced a group of five-year-olds to informational text structures during the daily read-aloud and circle time. Using the theme of dinosaurs, they selected the read-aloud texts and planned and taught the lessons. The teacher first met with the teacher-librarian to identify books on the topic of dinosaurs and sort them by text structure. Then, the teacher and teacher-librarian designed read-aloud learning activities with the selected books for each of the five text structures. Each learning activity was structured using the before, during, and after framework of a read-aloud. The partners planned five read-alouds to take place in the library with the teacher-librarian taking the major teaching role; however, the teacher also actively observed and supported the children. Specifically, the teacher reinforced and extended children's learning about text structures in the classroom through a variety of follow-up activities. The remainder of this chapter describes the five read-aloud experiences that took place in the library and the follow-up activities that took place in the classroom.

Introducing Question–Answer Text Structure

To begin the unit, the teacher and teacher-librarian planned an activity to explore what the children already knew about dinosaurs.

Question–Answer Text Structure Titles

What Did Dinosaurs Eat? And Other Things You Want to Know About Dinosaurs, by E. MacLeod

Dinosaurs, by J. Opperman

- **Before Reading:** Facts about dinosaurs were written on strips of paper. Some of the facts were true (e.g., Dinosaurs are extinct) and some of the facts were false (e.g., Dinosaurs ate cavemen). The strips of paper were put upside-down on the carpeted area. Each child in

Brony (Brontosaurus) family

the class was invited to pick one strip of paper, read the fact with teacher support as needed, and identify whether it was true or false. If there was general agreement from the rest of the class on that child's answer, then the strip of paper with the fact was taped onto a chart under *Yes* for true or *No* for not true. If consensus could not be reached on whether the fact was true or false, the strip of paper with the fact was taped to the chart under *Don't Know*. In this way the teacher and teacher-librarian were able to identify areas for the children to research—those facts categorized under *Don't Know*. The class identified three questions: What did dinosaurs eat? How big were dinosaurs? What was dinosaur skin like?

Having identified these questions, the teacher-librarian introduced the book, *What Did Dinosaurs Eat? And Other Things You Want to Know about Dinosaurs* by E. MacLeod. She showed the illustrations to the children and identified that information in the book was organized around questions and answers. The children identified the questions they had generated.

- **During Reading:** The teacher-librarian paused in her reading whenever the text provided an answer to one of the children's questions. In this way she engaged the children in searching the text for the answers to their questions and invited their responses.

- **After Reading:** The answers found in the information text were written on construction paper and pasted underneath the children's questions. The children in this class were at an emergent stage of reading and writing so responses to the questions were short and concise. For example, the following response was written under the question: What did dinosaurs eat?

  Dinosaurs ate raw meat and leaves.

- **Follow-up Activity:** The teacher-librarian and teacher wanted to extend the students' learning by having them represent what they had learned in a collaborative Big Book. The children worked in small groups to create pages for this "Dinosaur Question and Answer Book." Each group tackled one question, creating a page or pages that provided answers to that question. In general, the book consisted of detailed illustrations with some emergent writing. In addition, the teacher-librarian and teacher acted as scribes writing down information dictated by the children. This book became part of the school library.

Descriptive Text Structure Titles

The Big Golden Book of Dinosaurs, by I. Jenkins

Dinosaurs, by Gail Gibbons

The Colossal Book of Dinosaurs by Micheal Teitelbaum

Dinosaur, by S. Walker and S. Gray

Introducing Descriptive Text Structure

As part of the unit on dinosaurs, the teacher-librarian and teacher had arranged for the children to go on a field trip to a local geology museum that contained the fossil remains of a Lambeasaurus dinosaur. In preparation for this trip, the teacher-librarian read aloud an information book by Micheal Teitelbaum, *The Colossal Book of Dinosaurs*, which is based on a descriptive text structure. This particular information book includes a section that provides both detailed illustrations of the Lambeasaurus and facts about its habitat and life.

- **Before Reading:** The teacher-librarian told the children she wanted to find out as much as she could about the Lambeasaurus dinosaur: what it looked like, how big it was, and what it ate. She then led the children on a picture walk of the illustrations and gathered as much descriptive information as possible from this source. She entered the information on a chart.

- **During Reading:** The teacher-librarian read the Lambeasaurus section, pausing when additional descriptive information was given, inviting student responses and adding the information to the chart.

- **After Reading:** The teacher-librarian read the descriptive chart she and the class had created and reviewed how they had collected and recorded this descriptive information.

- **Follow-up Activity:** Upon returning to the classroom, the children created descriptive drawings or diagrams of the Lambeasaurus dinosaur. Some labeled their drawings.

Introducing Sequence Text Structure

At the geology museum, the children not only saw the Lambeasaurus fossil but also fossils of dinosaur eggs. The teacher and teacher-librarian decided that the life cycle of dinosaurs would provide an excellent opportunity for exploring the sequence text structure. The teacher-librarian selected *The Book of Dinosaurs: A Complete History* by R. Rossi because it included a chapter on the life cycle of dinosaurs, "Eggs, nests and baby dinosaurs."

- **Before Reading:** The teacher-librarian asked the children to look closely at the illustrations and predict how the dinosaurs might have begun life.

- **During Reading:** The teacher-librarian read the information selection without stopping.

- **After Reading:** The teacher-librarian repeated her question about how dinosaurs began life. She entered the children's answer, "As an egg," on line one of a graphic organizer she had prepared. She then asked, "What happened next?" The children responded, "They hatched!" This response was entered on line two. This question-and-answer discussion continued until the children had successfully identified the sequence of the dinosaurs' life cycle. The teacher-librarian read the sequenced text that she and the children had created and reviewed how sequenced information is organized.

Sequence Graphic Organizer

- 1. _____
- 2. _____
- 3. _____
- 4. _____
- 5. _____

- **Follow-up Activity:** Filled with new learning, the children then worked in groups in the classroom to create dioramas of the dinosaur's life cycle. Those children who were able, labeled each phase in the life cycle.

Introducing Compare/Contrast Text Structure

Given the children's fascination with the mighty flesh-eating Tyrannosaurus Rex, the teacher and teacher-librarian decided that it would be the ideal dinosaur to compare and contrast with the more gentle plant-eating Lambeasaurus. For the library read-aloud, the teacher-librarian selected the information book *Tyrannosaurus Rex* by S. Calver.

- **Before Reading:** The teacher-librarian reviewed what the children had learned about the Lambeasaurus dinosaur and asked some of the children to share their drawings and diagrams of the dinosaur. She then asked if all dinosaurs were the same. For example: Did they eat the same things? Were they of the same size? Did they all lay eggs? A lively discussion ensued and the teacher-librarian listed the children's ideas on a "T-chart" under *Same* and *Different*. She then introduced *Tyrannosaurus Rex*, showing the title and illustrations, and asked the children to listen for the ways in which the Tyrannosaurus Rex was the same as and the ways in which it was different from the Lambeasaurus.

- **During Reading:** The teacher-librarian paused whenever the text provided a particular detail about the Tyrannosaurus Rex that could be compared or contrasted with the Lambeasaurus. She asked the children whether that particular detail was the *same as* or *different from* the Lambeasaurus.

- **After Reading:** The teacher-librarian, in a "T-chart" developed with the children, recorded similarities and differences between the two types of dinosaurs.

- **Follow-up Activity:** At the mathematics table in the classroom, the children compared and contrasted models of dinosaurs and sorted them by similarities and differences. They were asked to record how they had categorized the model dinosaurs, for example, by diet or by size.

Introducing Cause and Effect Text Structure

At the end of the unit, the teacher and teacher-librarian planned to explore with the children what might have caused the extinction of the dinosaurs. Because the information book explores several ideas about what might have caused the extinction of the dinosaurs, they chose *What Happened to the Dinosaurs?* by F. M. Branley.

- **Before Reading:** The teacher-librarian reviewed with the children some of the information they had collected on the lives of dinosaurs. She then asked the children to predict why they thought dinosaurs might have become extinct and recorded their responses on chart paper. Finally, the teacher-librarian set the purpose for listening: to listen for ideas about why dinosaurs became extinct.

- **During Reading:** The teacher-librarian demonstrated comprehension strategies by stopping and thinking aloud whenever she encountered a new theory around why dinosaurs became extinct.

- **After Reading:** The teacher-librarian reviewed and discussed with the children what events (explored in *What Happened to the Dinosaurs?*) may have created the environmental changes that led to the dinosaurs' extinction. This information was entered on chart paper.

- **Follow-up Activity:** Returning to the classroom, the children were divided into four groups. Each group prepared and presented a short role-drama depicting an event which may have caused the dinosaurs' extinction:

    i) the destruction of dinosaur eggs by small animals which led to the hatching of only a few eggs
    ii) a group of dinosaurs getting sick and the sickness spreading to other dinosaur groups
    iii) a comet shower caused by the Nemesis star
    iv) a huge asteroid crashing into earth

Supporting Understandings of Informational Text Structures

In the space provided here, it is possible to provide only a sample of the many activities designed by the teacher and teacher-librarian to support young children's beginning understandings of informational text structures. Other activities designed for the classroom included writing and illustrating a dinosaur guidebook sequenced in alphabetical order; planning and creating dinosaur fossils from collected twigs (dinosaur bones) and comparing and contrasting these fossils with a human skeleton; and measuring and marking with tape on the classroom floor the Lambeasaurus dinosaur (approximately 15 metres) and the Compsognathus dinosaur (about the size of a hen). All of these activities built upon some aspect of informational text structure that had been introduced or reinforced during the daily read-aloud.

During read-alouds with information books, the teacher-librarian supported the children's understandings of text structure in these ways:

- *by scaffolding instruction:* The teacher-librarian provided clues and supports as children attempted to either identify or use a text structure.
- *by creating graphic organizers:* The teacher-librarian created frames to help children understand how information is or can be organized.

- *by demonstrating and modeling:* Through strategies like think-alouds, the teacher-librarian demonstrated and modeled how to identify the way in which information is organized.
- *by asking focused questions:* The teacher-librarian used focused questions to provoke thinking, check for comprehension, and invite children's reflections.

In short, the teacher and teacher-librarian carefully organized read-alouds around information books and provided many opportunities for children to build their understandings of the informational text structures. Together, they created a richer learning experience for the children than they could have alone.

Although the examples and experiences shared in this chapter were with Kindergarten students, they can be easily adapted to fit the context of most Grades 1 to 7 classes. For science and social studies activities, reading aloud an information book can provide a powerful "hook" to motivate children in exploring new topics. Reading short excerpts from journals or diaries can awaken interest and set the stage for a comprehensive unit of study. There is a wealth of informational literature for students on all imaginable topics, and teachers and teacher-librarians could read aloud science and social studies books to strengthen student comprehension of text structures. This strategy builds comprehension of text structures while engaging students in the content.

6

Teaching Reading Strategies to Build Information Literacy

Elizabeth A. Lee

How is it that some people seem to know about the best deals, the cheapest flights or the most efficient route across town? We all have such friends, the ones we turn to when we need information. You may be such a person.

What enables these individuals to be so knowledgeable? We may characterize these people as effective learners. But they are more than that. Whether it is the best source for a new computer or a reliable mechanic, these "information experts" have advanced skills in posing questions, locating and using information to achieve their goals. In educational terms, they are **information literate**. As defined by the American Library Association (1998), they are "able to recognize when information is needed and have the ability to locate, evaluate, and use effectively the needed information."

This chapter examines the teaching of information literacy, reviews models commonly used for organizing it, and sets information literacy in various contexts. Inherent in the concept of information literacy are the reading and writing skills taught in traditional literacy programs—*all* teachers teach reading, including teacher-librarians. When teacher-librarians help students with research projects, teaching effective online searching skills, how to write project reports, and other information-based activities, they are really teaching reading and writing within the context of information literacy.

Recognizing that successful instruction in information literacy requires an understanding of effective reading strategies, this chapter offers powerful reading strategies that teachers and teacher-librarians can easily apply. Short activities illustrate some of the strategies for increasing learners' competency with information literacy tasks. Included as well are examples of classroom resources that can be used by teachers and teacher-librarians, and samples of elementary student work.

Models of Information Literacy

Please take a moment to try and work through this information problem.

Activity: *Jot down how you would go about planning a family reunion. What is the process and what are some of the skills you need in order to fulfill it?*

You would likely list items such as the following:

- sending messages to all your relatives in one or more ways, which calls for use of information literacy and media skills (e-mail, regular mail, chat group, listserv)
- picking a location, which involves reading maps online or in print
- researching accommodation
- booking flights, which requires document reading
- compiling a family history—interviewing, audio or video; digitizing photos; using print or Web-based publishing programs
- setting up a database or spreadsheet

This list, which could be lengthy, encompasses integrating background knowledge with newly gathered information—the *content* component of information literacy; effectively applying the research and inquiry process—the *what* component of information literacy; and using technical skills in a variety of media—the *how* component of information literacy. This activity demonstrates the types of everyday situations we find ourselves in: situations that are rooted in a need for information and for the effective application of that information to solve problems, make decisions, or acquire new knowledge.

Many of us acquired these skills informally, from parents, in the community, and perhaps in school. When books were the main source of information and a book report or an essay using secondary sources the most common products, learning a set of library and research skills in school was enough. However, in today's increasingly technological society, and with the move to a knowledge-based economy, such a narrow approach will not suffice. To some day take their places in the job market, students will need to learn many information skills and the strategies necessary to apply those skills effectively. This need is shifting the traditional view of "doing research" in the library to a more pervasive understanding that information literacy must be a major part of the school curriculum. Consequently, teachers and teacher-librarians need to work together at all grade levels to incorporate information literacy into instruction and integrate it throughout the curriculum (AASL and AECT, 1998; Ontario Library Association, 1999).

Educators in North America are using several different systems to organize information literacy skills. These information literacy models help teachers and teacher-librarians integrate a set of learning processes and individual information skills into their core curriculum frameworks. They provide a clear set of learning outcomes for information literacy while giving teachers a process model to teach students a way to approach information problem-solving. Here is a brief sampling of common models.

The Research Quest: Becoming Information Literate

The Research Quest model includes five components:

- *focusing:* Students begin with a focus on the research process, the purpose, and audience for the research.
- *finding and filtering:* Once the topic is focused, students explore a variety of information sources, applying evaluation criteria, recording sources, and making notes.

- *working with information:* Students interpret, analyze, and synthesize ideas to make them their own. Issues of plagiarism and intellectual rights are emphasized here.
- *communicating:* Students learn to share what they have learned in effective ways.
- *reflecting:* Students consider how successful and effective they were and reflect on ways they could improve the work they did.

The model was developed by the British Columbia Teacher-Librarians Association and adopted by the B.C. Ministry of Education in 2001.

http://gladstone.vsb.bc.ca/library/research1.htm

Building Information Literacy (BIL)

This model is a complete information literacy model and an online planning tool for teachers and teacher-librarians. The process developed within BIL includes these stages: (1) planning, (2) gathering information, (3) processing the information, (4) organizing information, (5) creating new information, (6) sharing and presenting, and (7) evaluating products and processes. BIL, developed by the Prince Edward Island Department of Education, organizes dozens of information learning outcomes by key stages: Grades 3, 6, 9, and 12.

www.edu.pe.ca/bil

Information Studies, Grades K–12

Information Studies, developed by the Ontario School Library Association, aligns with the Ontario Core Curriculum. It organizes research and inquiry into four stages: (1) preparing for research, (2) accessing resources, (3) processing information, and (4) transferring learning. This model, too, breaks down the information skills and strategies by grade levels.

http://www.accessola.com/action/positions/info_studies/html/research.html

Big6: An Information Problem-Solving Process

Big6 is a major model used throughout the United States, influencing the curriculum in most states. Researchers and practitioners have found that successful solving of problems encompasses six stages with two sub-stages under each.

Stages in Problem Solving

1. Task Definition

1.1 Define the information problem.

1.2 Identify information needed in order to complete the task—to solve the problem.

2. Information Seeking Strategies

2.1 Determine the range of possible sources (brainstorm).

2.2 Evaluate the different possible sources to determine priorities, that is, the best sources.

3. Location and Access

3.1 Locate sources of information.

3.2 Find information within sources.

4. Use of Information

4.1 Engage the information in a source. In other words, read it, hear it, view it, and touch it.

4.2 Extract relevant information from a source.

5. Synthesis

5.1 Organize information from multiple sources.

5.2 Present the information.

6. Evaluation

6.1 Judge the product (effectiveness).

6.2 Judge the problem-solving process (efficiency).

More information on the Big6 model can be found at **http://www.big6.com/.**

Source: Adapted from The Big Six Associates, LLC., 2004.

The strength of all these models is the emphasis they place on approaching inquiry and research as situations and tasks requiring a problem-solving process. Effective learners are taught to view their environments as problem spaces to explore. They intentionally select reliable resources, assess those resources for accuracy and currency, and then use those resources in respectful ways to build their own new knowledge. The models show how critical thinking, problem solving, decision making, and ethical uses of information form the cornerstones of information literacy.

With such a framework in place, effective learners become skilled at transforming the information they find into new knowledge and thus, move beyond simply retelling (or worse, copying) information for the teacher. They are given a purpose for their inquiries and focus their work on mobilizing new information and applying it to "real world" contexts. They read, write, and think while they are engaged in these processes, and they rely heavily on their literacy skills to become effective knowledge transformers.

The Relationship between Information Literacy and Reading

Many students' difficulties in becoming information literate stem from weak or inadequate reading strategies. When confronted with authentic tasks that require them to apply information literacy skills, they cannot apply reading strategies as a tool for learning.

- As Michael Pressley writes in *Reading Instruction That Works*, effective reading is an active meaning-making process. Readers derive meaning from text when they engage in problem-solving thinking during reading (National Reading Panel, 2000). Information literacy, in the broadest sense, involves problem-solving. More specifically, in order to carry out information literacy tasks effectively, the mastery of specific reading skills is required.
- Some learners encounter difficulty with reading in Grades 4 to 7 because the focus shifts from learning to read to reading to learn; they now need to apply reading skills and strategies for learning and creating new information.
- Inadequate reading skills, particularly weak reading comprehension, prevents many children from effectively engaging in research. It is not necessarily an inability to locate information or to use various information literacy tools that causes the downloaded, full-of-undigested-ideas report. Rather, a lack of reading strategies is often to blame—if readers do not know how to ask questions of a text, do not comprehend it, perhaps using text structures, or cannot summarize it, they have no recourse but to copy.
- Building students' information literacy base requires that teachers and teacher-librarians work together to integrate instruction in reading strategies and information literacy into all areas of the curriculum (Lee, 2005).

Key Reading Strategies for Information Literacy

Three powerful strategies enable learners to engage with and use texts to solve a problem. They are the vehicle for the effective use of information. In *Teaching Children to Read*, the National Reading Panel reported that these three are particularly effective in improving readers' comprehension of text:

1. questioning
2. summarizing
3. using text structure clues

1. Questioning

Asking questions is the basis of problem solving and taking an intentional stance towards learning. Teachers' questions to students can aid students in linking their background knowledge to the text and lead to a deeper understanding. Questions can help students retain information. Playing a key role in instruction, they should be directed at different levels of thinking, as represented in Bloom's taxonomy: (1) knowledge, (2) comprehension, (3) application, (4) analysis, (5) synthesis, and (6) evaluation. One framework for questioning that is easily understood by students in the elementary grades and has also been successfully used at the secondary level is Question–Answer Relationship.

Question–Answer Relationship (QAR)

QAR is a framework that helps learners locate information in a text and answer questions by categorizing the possible sources of information. As T. E. Raphael confirms, teaching learners QAR will improve their comprehension of texts. The strategy makes the thinking and reading process transparent to learners and provides memorable labels that help direct the process. QAR scaffolds a reader's interaction with a text: it categorizes the possible sources of information needed in order to answer a question. This strategy may be used with narrative as well as informational text—it is a powerful tool for learning with informational text.

- Provide learners with an overview of the four categories of questions. Two categories can be described as in the text; the other two, in your head.

  1. *Right There questions:* The answer is easily found in the text.
  2. *Think and Search questions:* The answer is in the text, but the words may not be found in the same sentence.
  3. *Author and You questions:* The answer is found by putting together what you know with what you read in the text.
  4. *On Your Own questions:* The answer is not in the text. The answer will come from your own experience and knowledge.

- Using a set of prepared questions for a simple or familiar text, have readers answer the questions and decide through discussion the category to which each question belongs. The chart at the top of the next page shows typical word clues to look for.

Right There	Think and Search	In Your Head	On Your Own
What did	How do you	Why did	Have you ever
Who did	What are three or four	If you were a/an	If you could
How many			
What was	What happened to	What would you do if you	If you were going to
Who are	What happened before	Which character would you like to be? Why?	In your opinion
Define			Do you agree with . . . ? Why?
What does . . . mean?	What happened after	What part of the text made you angry? smile? sad? Why?	Do you know anyone who
What kind	How many times		How do you feel about
	What examples	What do you feel the author is trying to tell?	
	Where did		

This discussion is essential because it focuses the learners' attention on specific textual clues for comprehending the text.

- Provide students with practice in applying the categories to more sets of questions based on various types of text. Let them work in pairs and on their own.
- Once learners in Grades 4 to 7 are confident in applying the QAR system to provided questions, teach them to *generate* questions for a text applying the different question categories. Provide students with a short text of several paragraphs and model generating questions of each category for that text. Using a think-aloud, model for students how they can generate questions. For example, read the first paragraph and ask a couple of questions from the Right There category. "What did . . . ?" or "What does . . . mean?" Let them pick another one for that category and try it. Proceed through the text mixing think-alouds with guided practice until they can follow the procedure independently. Question generation puts much greater cognitive demands on the reader. Formulating a question that fits a specific category requires the reader to process the text deeply.
- Once learners have mastered the strategy, periodically review it and remind them to apply QAR while reading.

Two activities for applying QAR follow.

QAR Activity A: *A simple text. Activity A can be used to introduce the process through modeling, as described above. If you are unfamiliar with QAR, try categorizing the questions into the four categories. Answers appear below the questions.*

Jack and Jill
went up the hill
to fetch a pail of water.

Questions:

1. Who went up the hill?
2. Where was the water located?
3. What must be at the top of the hill?
4. What is the name for this type of story?

Answers:

1. Jack and Jill.
   Category: Right There (Answer is easily found in the text.)
2. At the top of the hill.
   Category: Think and Search (Answer is there but it must be found.)
3. A well, pond, or spring.
   Category: Author and You (Answer is found by combining personal knowledge with information in the text.)
4. Nursery rhyme
   Category: On Your Own (Answer is based solely on prior knowledge.)

QAR Activity B: *A short piece of expository text is provided for practice. After reading the text, try to generate a question based on the text for each category. Below is an example for each category, for which there will be multiple possibilities.*

Settling the Prairie

The prairie was open flat grassland that stretched for miles with few trees in the middle of the continent. Trees grew around the small number of rivers and creeks. The summer was shorter and hotter on the prairie and winters were colder and longer than back east. Settlers faced many challenges when the West was opened for farming. Many had never farmed, as they had worked as servants or in factories. A land claim often was not near a river. A settler had to build a house and live on the land claim for most of the year in order to earn title to the land. Many of the settlers' first houses were built of sod, the tough top layer of the grass. The settlers first had to break through the sod with a plow before they could make blocks to pile up to make walls. An early name for settlers was sodbusters. After building a house the settlers had to plant crops. Often, the crops failed.

Examples:

1. Right There: Where was the prairie located?
2. Think and Search: What are two things that made it hard for settlers to build homes?
3. Author and You: Why was it difficult to grow crops on the prairie?

4. On Your Own: Would you have wanted to be a settler?

Whether it is applying QAR to text as discussed above or generating questions in response to observations during a science experiment as below, questioning is central to learning. Both question-answering and question-generating enhance learning.

Day-by-Day Observations: Drosophila Cultures
Starting Day: February 29, 2004

Day 1: Everything seems to be doing well in every one of the tanks, except the cool one (15° C). The flies seem to be moving in slow motion, just kind of crawling around the bottom of the tank. The warm tank (25° C) seems to be doing really well. The flies seem to be flying around. The room temperature flies are doing about the same as the warm tank jar.

Day 2: The cool tank has a few dead flies in the bottom. The warm tank seems to be thriving. We noted that there were white tube-like things in the room temperature jar and warm jar. They move when in direct light, slowly and caterpillar-like.

Day 3: Not much change since yesterday. The cold jar has more dead ones, though.

Day 4: There are only a few flies in the cool jar. The warm and room temperature jars had about 25-30 larvae apiece today!

Day 5: There were a few dead flies in the warm jar today. <u>Maybe this means something?</u>

Day 6: There is only one living fly in the cool temperature jar. There were more larvae in the room temperature jar. <u>Could this possibly be from reproduction? Is this the end of their life cycle?</u>

Day 7: The room temperature jar seems to be doing extremely well, but that was expected, as this is their normal living conditions.

Day 8: The cold jar is dead. There are no more fruit flies left. When the lid was removed, all you could see was little corpses.

Day 9: The room temperature jar has more green larvae. <u>Is this a stage in the lifecycle? Are they air-deprived? Are they dead?</u> We have no answers yet.

Day 10: Today most of the healthy larvae are either brown or green.

Day 11: Today we noted that the larvae that were green yesterday had turned brown. <u>Does this mean they are dead?</u> On the other hand, <u>is it like a cocoon and they have hatched</u>? The room temperature jar has four new flies, however, and no brown shells. <u>What does this mean?</u>

(Courtesy of Shannon Donogh, Grade 9, Winnipeg, Manitoba)

2. Summarizing

Researchers consider summarizing the most effective comprehension strategy (Pressley, Johnson, Symons, McGoldrick & Kurita, 1989). In order to summarize, readers have to decide what is important, condense it, and put it into their own words. They process the text deeply, doing much more than a simple retell, which relies on literal recall and sequence of story events.

Constructing a summary while reading is a means of self-monitoring understanding and retaining content. It is a tool for learning content-area concepts from informational texts. As a complex skill, it requires explicit instruction combined with sufficient practice over many grades. Writing summaries is difficult for elementary school students so students should first be asked to summarize orally (Hidi & Anderson, 1987). Teachers can shape students' oral summarizing by asking questions that help them condense their information. Two examples follow.

1. In response to a primary child's oral recount of a family trip—full of many details and the repetitive phrase "and then we . . . "—the teacher could ask, "What were the two best things that you did?" The student might reply, "I went fishing and I got to stay up late." The teacher could then ask the student to tell the group about his trip in four sentences, summarizing where the family went, the two best things he did, and how the trip ended.

2. After the class has read a section in a science or social studies book, the teacher could take a paragraph and model how to give an oral summary. The teacher could then ask students to give oral summaries of other paragraphs from the text. If a student gives too detailed a summary—basically rereading the paragraph as is often the case in initial attempts at summarizing—the teacher could ask the student one of these questions: "What's the most important idea? What idea do we want to remember from this paragraph? What idea do we need to write down from this paragraph?" This scaffolding of oral summaries could be linked to writing instruction on paragraph structure and main ideas.

One of several systems for summarization is provided below. This one is derived from *Reason to Read*, volume 2, by C. C. Black and J. N. Mangieri.

A System of Summarization

1. Delete duplication.

Example: There was a rabbit and in the beginning he was really splendid. He was fat and bunchy as a rabbit should be.

Summary: The splendid rabbit was fat and bunchy.

2. Combine ideas with the same subject.

Example: He had a brown coat with white spots. He had thread whiskers and his ears were lined with pink satin. His spots made him stand out among the plain red stockings.

Summary: His brown coat, white spots, and pink-lined ears made him stand out among the plain red stockings.

3. Restate in fewer words.

Example: There were other things in the stocking, nuts and oranges, and a toy engine, and chocolate almonds, a mouse and candy canes, but the rabbit was the best of all.

Summary: The stocking was filled with Christmas treats, but the rabbit was the best gift.

4. Use summary words.

Example: Summary words include *almost all, in conclusion, in brief, the main point, on the whole, ultimately, to sum up.*

5. Remove details that are not about the main subject.

Example: On Christmas morning when he sat wedged in the top of the boy's stocking with a sprig of holly between his paws, the Velveteen Rabbit looked charming.

Summary: The Velveteen Rabbit looked charming.

Summarization Activity: *Apply the five steps to this sample text.*

For thousands of years, Panda bears have lived in China. Pandas eat bamboo which grows in valleys and on mountains. Today many of these valleys and mountains are being farmed. Now there is less land where bamboo can grow. Many people fear Pandas will die out as today there are fewer Pandas alive than in the past. They are studying the Panda's habits. People hope to find ways to save the Pandas and see their numbers grow.

Answer: Your summary will likely be similar to this: Chinese Panda bears are in danger of becoming extinct because of the loss of their habitat.

Summarizing is a complex skill that requires careful instruction and ample practice. It is an essential means of coping with an overload of information. It enables the learner to retain only the core information. Because it requires readers to shift through and transform ideas into their own words, it fosters deeper processing and meaning making from a text.

Responsible Use of Resources

The Panda bear selection offers the perfect chance to remind students about the issues associated with plagiarism: "Why can't I simply take a sentence from the text and call that my summary? Why do I have to rewrite it in my own words?" These are not easy questions to answer and yet in today's world of rapid and easy access to information, it is more important than ever to teach students to respect intellectual property and authors' rights. Of course, if the author is assigned credit and the author's words are quoted properly, the exact words may be used.

In a second lesson based on the Panda bear text, students could explore this question: Could I use these words as my summary?

> People hope to find ways to save the Pandas and see their numbers grow.

Yes, these words could be used because they sum up most of what the author is trying to say; however, the sentence must be set off in quotation marks and written exactly as shown in the text: "People hope to find ways to save the Pandas and see their numbers grow."

The teacher might say, "Do you remember when we talked about using quote marks? They show the exact words someone says. Here, they show the exact words someone wrote."

3. Using Text Structure Clues

Chapter 5 provides more information on text structures.

Text Structure Activity: *Read the paragraph below and think about what makes it easy or difficult for you to read.*

The Fall of the Roman Empire

Rome dominated much of the world for four hundred years. A number of factors caused it to fall. Early on, Rome had ruled the client nations by working with the local rulers. Because local rulers were delegated areas of authority, they were part of Rome's power structure and supported Rome. As a result of fearing threats from the provinces, the later Emperors ruled by oppression. By the third century, Rome came to depend upon barbarian armies; consequently, many barbarians settled within the empire, becoming an internal threat. In 330 A.D. the empire split into two, the western and eastern parts. This led to the wealthy eastern part refusing to pay for the defence of the western part.

Answer: Short sentences combined with a cause–effect text structure using many signal words helps make this text easy to read.

Well-organized text is easier to process, as the relationships between concepts are evident from the argument structure and the signal words used. Expert readers are more aware of expository text structure and use it to support their comprehension and recall. Learning about text structure can improve students' comprehension and memory of text (Berkowitz, 1986; Taylor, 1982). By helping students recognize a variety of text structures, teachers and teacher-librarians provide students with a strategy for learning.

Teaching of text structure can follow a logical structure, beginning with students' everyday experiences as expressed in their narratives. Effective teachers model how the events unfold in sequence and how the descriptive language helps the reader understand. Then, working with a short text, they can think aloud about it and have group discussions about explicitly labeling text structures—sequencing, description, comparing/contrasting, and cause–effect.

Signal words are important to consider because they provide many clues to text structure. To reinforce their role, cut up a paragraph that uses many signal words, mix the order up, and have students assemble it in the correct order, discussing how the signal words help identify the text structure. Common signal words and phrases are listed under common text structures in the chart below.

Signal Words

Sequence	Description	Comparison	Cause–Effect
on	to begin with	however	because
not long after	most important	but	since
now	also	as well as	therefore
as	in fact	on the other hand	consequently
before	for instance	not only . . . but also	as a result
after	for example	either . . . or	this led to
when		while	so that
first		although	nevertheless
second		unless	accordingly
next		similarly	if . . . then
then		yet	thus
finally			

Adapted from *Content Area Reading: Literacy and Learning across the Curriculum,* 6th edition, by R. T. Vacca and J. L. Vacca (New York: Longman, 1999).

A Way to Teach Text Structure

Once signal words, such as those on the chart, have been introduced to students, it is helpful if the teacher draws students' attention to them in texts during a guided reading lesson. Doing so refreshes students' memory and reminds them of how signal words aid comprehension.

With the students, discuss the structure of a familiar experience and through group discussion develop it in an outline form. For example, the group could sequence the school day on the chalkboard, underlining or circling the sequence signal words.

Next, students could independently write a sequence of their own choice, such as outlining their day after school or playing a sport, being sure to include several sequence words from the list. They might refer to a set of signal words previous introduced.

A teacher may use a short text and model, through a think-aloud, how to use the signal words and think about the structure, building up evidence to explicitly label it. For example, a teacher's think-aloud based on "The Fall of the Roman Empire," at the start of this section, might go as follows:

"When I'm reading, I want to look for signal words that help identify the type of text as that will help me figure out how the author's ideas are related to each other."

The teacher reads aloud the whole text once. Then, the teacher rereads, "Rome dominated much of the world for four hundred years. A number of factors caused . . ." The teacher stops reading at *caused*.

"I think it might be a cause–effect text since it has the word 'caused' early on. I'll read on to see if there are more of these types of signal words."

The teacher reads past the text about the fall of the empire. "Early on, Rome had ruled the client nations by working with the local rulers. Because . . ."

"OK, another signal word, 'because,' is telling me why local rulers supported Rome. They were part of its power structure."

The teacher then reads, "As a result of fearing threats from the provinces, the later Emperors ruled by oppression."

"Yes, now the text tells me things have changed and 'as a result' tells me why. This must be a cause–effect text. I'll read on and see if there are more signal words, though. Cause–effect texts explain why something happens, so there may be more."

The teacher continues to read aloud to the end of the text. If the text is on an overhead, she could reread and quickly ask students to identify the signal words while she underlines them—students thereby gain another exposure to the words in context. The teacher concludes by saying, "Looking back at the title 'The Fall of the Roman Empire,' I see I could have expected to find this text structure used. The title suggests that the text might be an explanation of why Rome fell."

It is also helpful if students are provided with graphic organizers that show the structure of the text. These can be used for taking notes from texts for research purposes or to help organize ideas for writing in a variety of curricular areas. Because they are visual, graphic organizers help learners organize and link relationships, and also, due to the restricted space provided, encourage students to extract the key points. The use of graphic organizers facilitates learning. (See the outline next page.)

Students use these structures not only for reading, but also in writing across the curriculum. The sample on the next page is the cover and one section of a social studies assignment from a Grade 4 class in which students were to compare and contrast two countries on one topic. After learning key concepts about the geography, economies, and societies of Canada and Japan as a class, students chose a topic for an independent research project. Sam chose sports as his topic and used the compare and contrast text structure to organize and write his report.

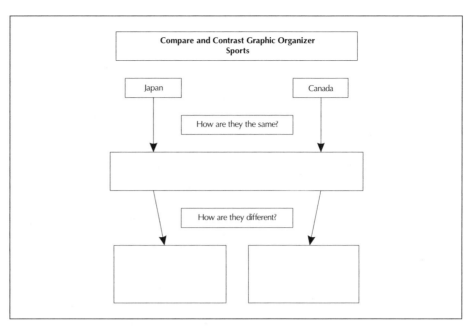

By giving students choice and engaging them in developing topics of personal interest, teachers help limit the temptation to simply copy information.

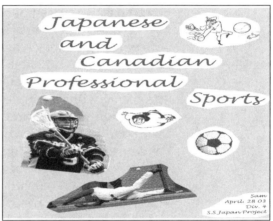

Wrestling or Sumo?

The style of wrestling in Japan is called sumo wrestling while in Canada the types of wrestling are freestyle and Greco-roman. In the sport of sumo wrestling the object is either to push your opponent out of the ring or make your opponent touch the floor with any other part of his body other than his feet. The rules are very simple: either sumo wrestler is not allowed to punch or kick the other person. That is the only real rule. In Greco-roman and freestyle wrestling in Canada both have a ring (just like sumo wrestling.) In sumo wrestling and in Greco-roman no holds are allowed to take place below the waist. But in freestyle and hold goes. As mentioned above, the traditional sumo wrestling in Japan has only two ways for a competitor to win (or one wrestler cheats.) While in Canada if you cheat (kick, punch or head butt) three times and the referee calls you, you are disqualified. Or the other way to win is if you pin your opponent for 3 seconds. The wrestling in Japan is very different from the wrestling in Canada.

(Courtesy of Sam Filipenko, Grade 4, Vancouver, British Columbia)

Helping Students Apply Reading Strategies

Teaching reading strategies is essential for the Information Age. Learners need an array of reading strategies to access and comprehend information to solve the learning problems they have at school and in their daily lives. Students need to be helped to move from simply reading a text to actively engaging with it in a problem-solving manner. The development of a repertoire of reading strategies will equip them to handle the literacy challenges in their lives.

Becoming skilled at using the strategies of questioning, summarizing, and text-structure enables students to more fully comprehend what they read. These strategies enable learners to ask effective questions, employ text structure as an aid to comprehension and retention, and extract relevant information from the multitude of sources available. The teaching of these strategies, along with others (see the National Reading Panel, 2000), helps students become active problem solvers. In other words, they become knowledge transformers, not just knowledge tellers.

Knowledge transformers read for their own purposes and create their own texts. When a student engages in knowledge transformation, there is less chance that plagiarism will occur. As noted earlier, plagiarism is often the result of lacking the strategies to understand a text well enough to put text ideas into one's own words.

Strategies and information literacy skills enable students to address problems within complex learning environments. By collaborating for instruction, teachers and teacher-librarians can better provide students with opportunities to acquire the knowledge and skills to become information experts. Instruction in reading strategies and information literacy skills is best embedded in curricular tasks. It involves systematically modeling strategies with a variety of genres across curricular areas, linking the use to success in comprehension. Ultimately, it can lead to students understanding and using information for their own learning goals.

7

Exploring Online Learning Resources

Richard Beaudry

Every day, in classrooms all over North America, students search for information and resources needed for school and homework assignments. Until 1990, most available resources would have been found in the classroom, school library, or public library. That year, the concept of accessing information went from a local to a global perspective: Tim Berners-Lee, from the W3 Consortium, wrote the first Web browser and server programs. These programs were written to simplify viewing and storing information on the Internet. This capability, in turn, opened the door for the exchange of information online using hypertext and hypermedia formats—the Internet was transformed from a static source of information to an interactive tool for teaching and learning. According to Internet World Statistics, by 2004, the Internet reached more than 800 million people in 190 countries; it is growing every day.

With the arrival of Web browsers, searching the voluminous amount of information and resources posed a singular challenge: How do we find the information? How do we store the information so we can access it quickly again? The Online Computer Library Center estimates that there are "between 3 and 8 billion pages currently available on the public web" (IMSA, 2002).

The challenge of finding these resources required creating software that could sift quickly through cyberspace to seek out and find available information; as a result, in 1994, the first search engines—Yahoo, WebCrawler, and Lycos—appeared. **Search engines** are programs accessible through Web browsers (e.g., Explorer and Netscape) that seek information based on specific criteria entered by the user. They use a variety of descriptors and keywords for locating Web sites. There are two types:

- individual search engines (e.g., Google at **http://www.google.ca** or Yahoo at **http://ca.yahoo.com/**) that have their own databases of indexed Web sites
- meta-search engines (e.g., Clusty at **http://clusty.com/** or Dogpile at **http://www.dogpile.com/**) that search databases from other search engines and post the results

To find information, students and teachers query the search engine and it searches its database for possible links.

Other problems have arisen within the competing search engines available:

- Web sites may not be active.
- Updates depend entirely on the company or institution running the search engine.

- The indexing of each search engine database is based on different keywords.
- Search engines cannot keep pace with the increasing number of Web sites.
- Searches can result in thousands of hits. Many of the top search engines post commercial links on their first page, although these may not be the best results for the search.

The Teaching Potential of Technology

Wider and faster access to the Internet prompted school districts in North America to invest in computer technology throughout the 1990s. To reflect this investment, curriculum guides were updated to assist teachers in teaching information technology and information literacy skills to students. Before the introduction of technology in schools, teacher-librarians were mainly responsible for managing collections, finding in-school resources for staff and students, and running reading or literacy programs; since the advent of technology, they have taken a leadership role in teaching information literacy skills to both teachers and students.

Using appropriate online resources requires a greater level of collaboration between teachers and teacher-librarians who teach information literacy skills to students and help teachers in finding the best resources. A key issue in the use of online resources is assessing their content and appropriateness for use with elementary students. Teacher-librarians use a variety of criteria for evaluating Internet resources based on five areas:

- authority (Who created the Web site?)
- accuracy (Is the information on the Web site correct?)
- bias (Does the Web site offer more than one viewpoint?)
- currency (When was the Web site last updated?)
- coverage (Is the information on the Web site complete?)

Carolyn Ledwell, a teacher-librarian in Prince Edward Island, adapted a tool created by *School Libraries in Canada* for use with teachers and students. The tool, which appears as "Criteria for Evaluating Internet Resources" on pages 117–18, is helpful when teachers and teacher-librarians are selecting Web sites for use on student projects and designing lessons so students can evaluate Web sites independently.

Recent research shows that *how* technology is used in schools today depends more on the teaching experience and interest of the teacher in using technology rather than any standards set out in curriculum guides. In 2003, the National Association of State Boards of Education surveyed computer and Internet use by teachers. It found that "Eighty-two percent of teachers cited a lack of release time for training as the greatest barrier to using computers or the Internet for instruction. As would be expected, teachers in general reported feeling more prepared to use technology as the number of hours of training increased."

How is technology being used in our schools? Teachers are certainly using it, but not always for specific teaching purposes. David Bowman, in "Thinking through the Technology Puzzle," observed, "A significant percentage of teachers use technology for their personal needs but don't employ it in the classroom." This raises the challenge for all educators. It also further supports the idea that teacher-librarians and classroom teachers should work together to plan for effective uses of Web resources. For example, when planning a unit on government, a Grade 5 teacher and teacher-librarian could collaboratively select Web sites for students to use during the unit, call for students to use two search engines to compare the information found on each, and ask students to identify the most reliable sources of information on government.

Showcasing Digital Learning

The results of a typical online search can be daunting. Using one of the many popular search engines could easily yield more than a million "hits," and reading through the results can be time consuming without yielding information that teachers and students can use. This problem points to the need for all teachers and learners to develop effective search skills.

In their daily role of finding resources, both in print and online, teacher-librarians have always been information specialists. When working in collaboration with the classroom teacher, teacher-librarians recommend all types of resources, including Web sites that complement a unit of study. It is now possible to find digital resources for just about any lesson plan from Kindergarten to Grade 12. Once these are found, teachers can integrate these resources into student learning.

In addition, for teachers and teacher-librarians who want to learn more about using technology in their teaching, there are several Internet sites addressing the issue of learning with technology. By offering online tutorials and resources, government, educational, and institutional Web sites give teachers and students online resources such as these:

- tutorials that can teach information literacy skills
  (e.g., The Texas Information Literacy Tutorial at
  http://tilt.lib.utsystem.edu/intro/issues.htm and Information
  Overload at Stanford University's
  http://ldt.stanford.edu/~pworth/ed124x/searchy/Main.html)
- information portals that offer a wide variety of resources
  (e.g., School Library Information Portal at **http://www.cla.ca/slip/**
  and Awesome Library at **http://www.awesomelibrary.org/**)
- education resource centres that work with teacher education programs and have links to new literacies
  (e.g., the University of British Columbia's Language Education
  Resource Centre at **http://www.lerc.educ.ubc.ca/LERC/** and the
  University of Prince Edward Island's Education Resource Centre at
  http://www.upei.ca/~fac_ed/html/erc.html)
- interactive Web sites that offer curriculum guides and lesson plans
  (e.g., *The Centre for Teaching History with Technology* at
  http://thwt.org/ and the *Teacher's Corner Lesson Plans* at
  http://www.theteacherscorner.net/resources/websites.htm)

In response to the curriculum demands of their own school, many teacher-librarians have created school library Web sites that showcase the best resources for supporting current unit plans and assisting students in projects and homework. School library Web sites also showcase exemplars of student projects, as well as collaboratively planned activities and units by teachers and teacher-librarians. These exemplars include student writing, drawings, photographs of completed projects, and reactions and comments from students on how they much they enjoyed the project.

The school library Web site of the Prince of Wales Secondary School, in Vancouver, British Columbia, is a good model of what a teacher-librarian, working in collaboration with classroom teachers, can offer in online resources. Begun in 1996 by teacher-librarian Karen Cordiner, the Web site offers online resources and learning activities that support the B.C. curriculum. Teachers can search by content or subject matter. The site is updated regularly and the teacher-librarian continues to work with teachers in finding appropriate resources to add to the site.

http://pw.vsb.bc.ca/library/index.htm

Whitehorse Elementary, situated in Yukon Territory, has an exemplary Web site of the collaborative work that can be done by classroom teachers, computer teachers, and teacher-librarians. Like the Prince of Wales Library Web site, the Whitehorse site offers many Web links and ideas for teachers based on subjects or themes taught in the school. It also showcases online student projects and offers WebQuests, created collaboratively by the staff and teacher-librarian.

http://www.yesnet.yk.ca/schools/wes/webquest_collection.html
http://www.yesnet.yk.ca/schools/wes/

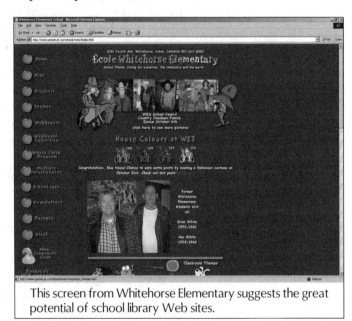

This screen from Whitehorse Elementary suggests the great potential of school library Web sites.

Another Web site worth mentioning is that created by the Calgary Board of Education's Media Services. Serving all elementary teacher-librarians in the district, it has links to subject areas, access to the online union catalogue for the district, an online book club (Wired for Words), and a section called "Ask a Teacher-librarian" where students, teacher-librarians, teachers, library support staff, and parents can seek support for finding resources and information.

http://schools.cbe.ab.ca/curriculum/library/elementary/ elementary1.html

Below are examples of U.S. school library Web sites that offer a wealth of useful information. They exemplify how the teacher-librarian can archive the best relevant resources found online.

- The Bessie Chin High School Library Centre in Redwood, California: **http://rhsweb.org/library/**
- The Chico High School Library in Chico, California: **http://dewey.chs.chico.k12.ca.us/**
- The Springfield Township High School Virtual Library in Erdenheim, Pennsylvania: **http://mciunix.mciu.k12.pa.us/~spjvweb/**

All of these Web sites represent years of work from dedicated teacher-librarians who, in many cases, were self-taught in how to use the technology and software required to launch and maintain the sites. They act as models for other schools to create centralized online banks of resources connected to the school curriculum. They help teachers and students with their literacy learning and act as an access point for parents who want to help children with homework or learn more about what their children are learning. With the integration of technology in teaching, newer Web sites are being launched in a collaborative effort between the teacher-librarian, computer teacher, and classroom teachers.

What makes these Web sites successful?

- Committed teacher-librarians update the information regularly.
- The sites can be searched by content or subject area.
- The work of teachers and students is showcased.
- The sites provide access to reference materials that support curriculum guides.
- Parents and students at home can find resources and information.

Peter Millbury's Network of School Librarian Web Pages For a comprehensive look at school library Web sites from around the world, check this site out. It offers hundreds of Web links to school libraries in Canada, the United States, and in more than 20 countries around the world.

http://www.school-libraries.net/

Interactive Teaching Resources

Today, many educational Web sites offer interactive teaching tools for teachers and students. **Interactive Web sites** offer more than text and animations: they allow students and teachers to participate in online activities that can be in the form of games, tests, maps, video and audio components. Using search engines, collaborating with the teacher-librarian, or simply asking a colleague can yield some great examples of interactive Web sites.

The following examples feature digital resources that should be considered as useful links for school Web sites. Not only are they interactive; many offer teachers and teacher-librarians units of study to complement existing study guides.

Virtual Museums

Museums probably offer the best instance of the successful integration of multimedia and Internet access. Museums from around the world can now be accessed individually—see, for example, Vancouver Art Gallery at **http://www.vanartgallery.bc.ca/home.cfm** or the Canadian Museum of Contemporary Photography in Ottawa, at **http://cmcp.gallery.ca/**—or through indexed Web sites available online:

- *Virtual Library Museums Pages* has links to museum Web sites from around the world: **http://icom.museum/vlmp/**
- *MuseumSpot* is part of the StartSpot Network, through which searches can be done by country, city, museum name, and specialty: **http://www.museumspot.com/**

Museums, such as the Canadian Museum of Civilization (CMC) and the Smithsonian in Washington, D.C., present a wide variety of resources, but others, such as the Royal Tyrrell Museum (RTM) in Drumheller, Alberta, cover specific subjects such as dinosaurs in the Alberta Badlands.

CMC: **http:// www.civilization.ca/indexe.asp**
RTM: **http://www.tyrrellmuseum.com/**

The Smithsonian Institution and the Virtual Museum of Canada are two examples of Web sites that offer significant digital resources for teachers.

Virtual Museum of Canada (VMC)/Musée Virtuel du Canada (MVC): Rich in content and resources, the VMC is the result of collaboration between the Canadian government, heritage institutions, and hundreds of museums across the country. Their aim is to showcase Canada's rich and varied heritage using the power of the Internet. For educators, the VMC offers thematic lesson plans, exercises, games, and virtual exhibits for K–12 students. The VMC is a gateway to museums across Canada and visitors are invited to continue their journeys of discovery by traveling to the various museums that have contributed to this online project. Resources are accessible in both English and French.

http://www.virtualmuseum.ca/English/index_flash.html
http://www.museevirtual.ca/Francais/index_flash.html

The Smithsonian: The Smithsonian Institution has information and links to scientific, historical, and artistic resources from across the United States. The Smithsonian offers online access and resources to 15 affiliated U.S.

museums and organizations, each with its own Web site linked to the main homepage. Each affiliated Web site is interactive and showcases the contents and activities of the museum or organization.

The Smithsonian is the biggest institution of its kind in the world and through its Web sites aims to educate and entertain visitors with virtual tours. To facilitate teaching, a separate Web site has lesson plans, educational resources, and publications for K–12 teachers. Some resources are free to use while others are available for purchase. Although, ideally, every student should have an opportunity to visit the institution, the Web sites are a good substitute for teachers and students. The Smithsonian would be a useful link to add to any school library Web sites.

http://www.si.edu/
http://www.smithsonianeducation.org/educators/

Online Atlases

Interactive maps have benefited the teaching of geography from Kindergarten to Grade 12. Simple programs help students learn about their neighborhoods and ways to travel from one place to another. These include

- *Mapquest*: **http://www.mapquest.com/**
- *Rand McNally Get a Map*: **http://www.randmcnally.com/rmc/directions/dirGetMapInput.jsp?cmty=0**

Some organizations offer thematic maps that cover everything from population growth to transportation. Good examples include

- *National Geographic*: **http://www.nationalgeographic.com/maps/**
- *Atlapedia Online*: **http://www.atlapedia.com/**

To date, two national atlases have been converted to digital resources. Other countries and Web sites offer maps of various countries, but not with the in-depth coverage of the Atlases of Canada and the United States.

The Atlas of Canada/L'Atlas du Canada: The Atlas of Canada online provides a comprehensive collection of maps and related information about Canada. Launched by Canada's Ministry of Natural Resources in 1998, the Atlas lets students and teachers study interactive thematic maps and integrate them into existing unit plans. The Atlas is also available in French for francophone and immersion programs.

http://atlas.gc.ca/english/index.html
http://atlas.gc.ca/site/francais/index.html.document_view

NationalAtlas.gov: The U.S. Department of the Interior launched this Web site in 1998. It offers online maps, printable wall maps, interactive maps, and thematic maps. Teachers and students looking for information on climate, the environment, agriculture, government, history, transportation, and people will find the necessary resources to produce a map that can be viewed on a computer or downloaded and printed. Added bonuses are the interactive lessons for students to learn how to use the Web site tools.

http://nationalatlas.gov/natlas/Natlasstart.asp

These two online atlases are very practical tools for teachers and teacher-librarians. Most schools might have only one or two copies of these atlases so online access offers students information that can be viewed and downloaded from school and home in multiple copies. Both online versions are updated regularly with new information. The atlases should be considered as links to school library Web sites.

Google Earth: Launched in 2005, this interactive map program, with three levels of sophistication, takes advantage of satellite technology and uses 3D imagery to allow users to zoom in from space to their own neighbourhoods.

http://earth.google.com/index.html

Online Reference Tools

Online reference tools—online atlases, encyclopedias, almanacs, dictionaries, and more—are key resources for teachers and students. Teacher-librarians are always on the lookout for this type of resource since it provides a vast amount of information packed into one Web site. With limited library budgets, teacher-librarians need digital reference resources that can replace aging printed materials. Early on, most online reference Web sites had a cost attached to them and required a school licence and password to access the information. Although some still do, there are enough free online reference tools to complement students' research. Three key online reference tools are Factmonster, Awesome Library, and Bartleby.com.

Factmonster: Factmonster is an online atlas, almanac, dictionary, and encyclopedia all wrapped together and ready for use in schools. Factmonster offers many interesting resources for teachers and students who need up-to-date information. Two valuable sections for teachers and students are the Homework Center and a page on how to cite various types of resources. Other Web sites offer such tools, but those on Factmonster are easy to access and offer explanations that are simple to understand and follow.

http://www.factmonster.com/index.html

Awesome Library: Dr. Jerry Adams began developing this Internet reference in 1995. In 1997, the Evaluation and Development Institute began offering the links and resources through the Awesome Library Portal. Awesome Library now contains more than 26,000 carefully reviewed resources for K–12 schools. The Web site is divided into 24 thematic sections that offer links to Web sites that have been researched, evaluated, and indexed for content and use. Awesome Library offers links and resources in several languages—Spanish, French, German, Russian, Greek, Indonesian, Italian, Portuguese, Chinese, Korean, and Japanese. It has different levels of access for schools: teachers, children, teens, parents, librarians, and college students.

http://www.awesomelibrary.org/

Bartleby.com: This U.S.-based online reference, launched in 1999, encompasses general resources such as *The Columbia Encyclopedia,* 6th edition, *American Heritage Dictionary of the English Language,* 4th edition, and *Bartlett's Familiar Quotations*; it also provides specialized resources on religion, mythology, literary history and literature, anatomy, cooking, etiquette, and government.

http://bartleby.com/

These Web sites have long track records online, a measure of their usefulness to educators. Although many Web sites come and go, these are constantly updated sites are still offering valuable resources.

A distinctly Canadian encyclopedia also serves as a reference resource:

The Canadian Encyclopedia Online/L'encyclopédie canadienne: As "the most comprehensive and authoritative source of information on all things Canadian," this encyclopedia should be considered an important resource for social studies teachers. It has a comprehensive index of subjects and a wealth of information for teachers and students.

http://www.thecanadianencyclopedia.com/
index.cfm?PgNm=HomePage&Params=A1
http://www.thecanadianencyclopedia.com/
index.cfm?PgNm=HomePage&Params=F1

News Resources

Teachers and students are always on the lookout for up-to-date information on current events. Canadians and Americans can access a wide variety of radio or television resources from major news organizations. Canadian students have a distinct opportunity in viewing video news: *Connectivity and Learning in Canadian Schools* from Statistics Canada (2004) states, "An overwhelming majority (86%) of schools used broadband technologies to access the Internet."

CBC/Radio Canada: The Canadian Broadcasting Corporation, Canada's national public broadcaster, offers audio and video resources on national and international news, business, sports, health, science, and the arts. Radio Canada, the French language counterpart, offers similar audio and video resources.

http://www.cbc.ca/
http://www.radio-canada.ca/index.shtml

CTV News: As the leading video broadcaster in Canada, CTV offers online resources through Web sites that include **TSN.ca** (sports), **RDS.ca** (sports in French), **robtv.com** (business), and **discoverychannel.ca** (science).

http://www.ctv.ca/home

Canada.com network: This news resource offers newspaper, television, and online content from some of Canada's major news sources, including the *National Post*, the *Ottawa Citizen*, BCTV, the *Montreal Gazette*, and the *Vancouver Sun*.

http://www.canada.com/national/index.html

Canadian Press (CP): CP is the premier news gathering service for the Canadian press. It shares its news stories with more than 600 newsrooms across Canada and around the world.

http://www.cp.org/english/hp.htm

Associated Press (AP): Established in 1848, AP is the oldest news organization in the world. It sends out daily news items, photos, and audio and video feeds to more than one billion people.

http://www.ap.org/

CNN (Cable News Network): CNN.com has a staff of 4,000 news professionals stationed around the globe. End-users can access live video and audio, searchable archives and background information. CNN is the first news organization to present news on television 24 hours a day.

http://www.cnn.com/

MSNBC: MSNBC.com is a joint venture of Microsoft and NBC News. They allow end users to access the news and information 24 hours a day on the Internet and on cable television.

http://www.msnbc.msn.com/

Headline Spot: Its resources include news by media, by region, and by subject. Headline Spot is another branch of the StartSpot Network.

http://www.headlinespot.com/

In an era of globalization, access to news agencies from around the world is important so that students can view different perspectives on news items. North Americans typically focus on issues that affect their relationships with other countries and miss out on news items that may be important in Europe, Africa, Asia, or Oceania. News agencies on other continents present in-depth reviews of matters that concern their local populations. Students in courses like Comparative Civilization would benefit from seeing how the world looks at North Americans.

European News Resources

BBC News: This resource is the news arm of the British Broadcasting Corporation.

http://news.bbc.co.uk/

Reuters: Established in 1851, Reuters is the oldest news organization in Europe. It has 15,000 staff members in 91 countries around the world.

http://today.reuters.com/news/default.aspx

RTE: Radio Telefís Éireann is the Irish Public Service Broadcasting Organization.

http://www.rte.ie/

Oceania News Resources

ABC: The Australian Broadcasting Corporation is Australia's national, non-commercial broadcaster.

http://www.abc.net.au/news/

TVNZ: TV New Zealand is that country's public broadcaster.

http://www.tvnz.co.nz/

African News Resource

All Africa News: It is the largest online distributor of African news and information worldwide. Based in Mauritius, it has local offices in Johannesburg, Dakar, Lagos, and Washington, D.C.

http://allafrica.com/

Asian News Resources

Kyodo News, Japan: Kyodo is a nonprofit cooperative organization. It supplies political, financial, business, city, and cultural news from Asia and the Pacific Rim to non-Japanese media.

http://home.kyodo.co.jp/

Press Trust of India (PTI): This non-profit cooperative is owned by India's newspapers. Major TV and radio stations in India and several abroad access news items from it. PTI has a staff of 400 journalists and 80 news bureaus across the country and in foreign markets.

http://www.ptinews.com/pti/ptisite.nsf

Xinhuanet, China: It offers news coverage 24 hours a day in seven languages—Chinese, English, French, Spanish, Russian, Arabic, and Japanese.

http://www.xinhua.org/english/index.htm

RSS (Really Simple Syndication) catalogues headlines, making them readily available to consumers on the Internet. Teachers and students can use RSS to peruse major news stories and read items related to their studies. RSS is more effective than search engines for finding news on the Internet. At the time of publication, it had limited availability in Asia and Africa. Some RSS feeds:

All Africa: **http://allafrica.com/tools/headlines/rss.html**

Australian Broadcasting Corporation (ABC): **http://www.abc.net.au/news/services/default.htm**

BBC: **http://news.bbc.co.uk/1/hi/help/3223484.stm**

CBC: **http://www.cbc.ca/rss/**

CNN: **http://www.cnn.com/services/rss**

Kyodo: **http://home.kyodo.co.jp/modules/fstRSSFeed/index.php**

MSNBC: **http://www.msnbc.msn.com/id/5216556/**

Radio Canada: **http://www.radio-canada.ca/rss/**

Reuters: **http://today.reuters.com/rss/newsrss.aspx**

RTÉ: **http://www.rte.ie/webfeeds/**

Xinhuanet: **http://www.xinhuanet.com/english/rss_eng.htm**

Podcasting allows people with computers to record and post their own radio shows on the Internet and have them downloaded to any MP3 player. MP3 music players have been around since the mid-1990s, but it took Apple's IPod in 2001 to start a revolution with transportable hard drives capable of downloading gigabytes of music files; not long after, the concept of Podcasting was born. Radio news broadcasters, such as the Australian and Canadian Broadcasting Corporations, now offer selections of their radio programs to be accessed online and downloaded. People can then listen to these shows at their own leisure. The technology is still considered new so Podcasts are not as readily available as RSS feeds, but there are nearly 6,500 Podcast programs available to download on the Internet. Information on available Podcasts can be found at

- **http://www.podcastalley.com/**
- **http://www.ipodder.org/**
- **http://www.podcastingnews.com/**

Some examples:

ABC Podcasts: **http://www.abc.net.au/services/podcasting.htm#rn**
CBC Podcasts: **http://www.cbcradio3.com/podcast.cfm**
CNN Podcasts: **http://www.cnn.com/services/podcasting/**

Statistical Resources

Teachers and students looking for statistical information on the Internet can find useful government resources in Canada and the United States. In Canada, most statistical information can be found and downloaded from one central agency, Statistics Canada; however, in the United States, several federal and state agencies publish information and statistics on life in America.

StatsCan: Statistics Canada, based at **http://www.statcan.ca/**, has numerous resources for the general public and educators. High school students and teachers will find these StatsCan resources of particular interest:

- *Canada e-Book*, which "uses sound, images, tables, graphs and both analytical and descriptive text to look at Canada—The Land, The People, The Economy and The State" **http://142.206.72.67/r000_e.htm**
- Canada at-a-glance, a free document which "presents the current Canadian demographic, education, health, justice, housing, income, labour market, economic, travel, financial, and foreign trade statistics"
- lesson plans: **http://www.statcan.ca/english/kits/courses/list.htm**
- learning resources: **http://www.statcan.ca/english/ edu/list.htm**
- Canada's population clock: **http://www.statcan.ca/ english/edu/clock/population.htm**
- Census at school: **http://www19.statcan.ca/r000_e.htm**
- E-Stat, which "is a dynamic interactive teaching and learning tool for the education community" (Schools are required to have a licensing agreement to use it.) **http://www.statcan.ca/english/Estat/licence.htm**
- teachers' kits: **http://www.statcan.ca/english/kits/kits.htm**
- a French version of its Web site with the same resources available to teachers and students in francophone and French immersion schools **http://www.statcan.ca/start_f.html**

Beyond these services, StatsCan offers tutorials on finding and using resources, educational bulletins sent by e-mail to individuals and educational listservs, and The Daily, Statistics Canada's official public release bulletin which offers a comprehensive review of new information available.

Fedstats: As a U.S agency, found at **http://www.fedstats.gov/**, it is a good place to start looking for information and statistics on life in the United States. Fedstats offers links to more than 100 federal agencies that gather statistical information. As a search engine, it is linked to all agencies to find appropriate documentation and statistics. Each associated agency updates its database twice monthly to facilitate effective searches. There are more than 400 topics to search. A special feature, Mapstats, can be used to profile state, country, or congressional districts. Finally, the site provides access to statistical summaries from the departments of agriculture, education, energy, environment, health, income, labour, national accounts, safety, and transportation.

A final statistical resource worth mentioning is a United Nations Web site produced by the Department of Economic and Social Affairs. Found at **http://unstats.un.org/unsd/default.htm**, it provides information from the Statistics Division, which "compiles statistics from many international sources and produces global updates, including the Statistical Yearbook, World Statistics Pocketbook and yearbooks in specialized fields of statistics. It also provides to countries, specifications of the best methods of compiling information so that data from different sources can be readily compared."

Author Resources

Many authors have taken advantage of the Internet to post Web sites to communicate with their readers, promote their books, and announce upcoming releases. The Web site of J. K. Rowling, author of the Harry Potter books (**http://www.jkrowling.com**), and that of Jan Brett, an author and illustrator of children's books (**http://www.janbrett.com**), are good examples of popular interactive sites. It is possible to search online for individual authors, but for teachers and teacher-librarians, accessing online databases that provide information and resources on a number of children's authors is simpler. The Canadian Children's Book Centre and the Reading Room are two excellent examples.

The Canadian Children's Book Centre (CCBC): Launched in 1998, this Web site was created to promote Canadian books for children and teens. Well organized and easy to navigate, it provides resources for teachers, public and school librarians, students, and parents. The CCBC offers programs and resources that cover all aspects of Canadian children's literature, including special bibliographies, biographies, and teacher guides. It is a comprehensive and useful database.

http://www.bookcentre.ca/

The Reading Room: Linda Bertrand, a teacher-librarian who is well known throughout the United States and Canada for her work on Web sites with content for teacher-librarians, maintains this site. It is divided into several sections: Cool Kid's Sites, General Children's Literature Websites, Award Sites, Genres, Reading Lists, History of Children's Literature, Journals and Research in Children's Literature, Multicultural Literature and Young Adult Books. The site is updated regularly and all the hyperlinks work. The Reading Room is a good starting point for learning about children's literature published in the United States.

http://www.sldirectory.com/libsf/booksf/kidsbooks.html

Other Useful Book Resources

BookSpot: Another Web site from StartSpot Network, BookSpot is a one-stop Web site where teachers and students can access information and resources on books.

http://www.bookspot.com/

Carol Hurst's Children Literature Site: This site has information on children's authors and illustrations and resources for author studies, genre studies, and independent reading in the classroom or school library.

http://www.carolhurst.com/index.html

Teaching Books: Besides information on children's authors and illustrators, this site offers teacher guides and classroom materials on authors. The site is aimed at teachers and teacher-librarians preparing literature units on folktales, fairytales, and genre studies.

http://www.teachingbooks.net

Supporting the Information Literate Student

Information literacy involves dozens of skills and strategies that students develop over their schooling years. Curriculum guidelines across North American schools provide teachers with learning outcomes pertaining to defining an information question; using search tools to find appropriate resources; assessing the relevance of resources; and incorporating the results in assignments or presentations.

Defining the Question

Once a teacher starts work on an assignment or project with students, teacher-librarians teach students how to refine keywords so they can find the resources that they need and how to critically evaluate resources. Using provincial or state curriculum guides, as well as district information and communication technologies (ICT) guidelines, teacher-librarians help teachers integrate the information learning outcomes into student learning.

Finding Appropriate Resources

According to the July 2005 Nielsen NetRatings published in SearchEnginewatch.com, the three main search engines on the Internet—Google, Yahoo and MSNBC—are accountable for more than 80 percent of Internet searches (see **http://searchenginewatch.com/reports/article .php/2156451**).

Given these statistics, it makes sense to focus on Web site evaluation tools rather than a review of search engines. This is the perfect time to do a mini-lesson on evaluating the Web sites students find. Since the Internet is now a major resource for students in schools, they need to understand how to evaluate the information they find and how it will best serve their needs. To become information literate, they will need practice in evaluating Web sites and the tools to do so.

The Media Awareness Network is a good place to start looking for resources related to teaching with technology. The Web site offers

- more than 300 lesson plans
- professional development resources
- tips, information, and practical tools for parents
- an ever-expanding database of articles, research, reports, and other reference materials on current and emerging media issues

http://www.media-awareness.ca

Kathy Schrock, from Discoveryschool.com, is a valuable resource. She has been promoting critical evaluation skills for students by introducing the ABCs of Web site evaluation. Her Web site has several examples of Web site evaluation sheets. (See **http://school.discovery.com/schrockguide/evalu.html**.)

See "Criteria for Evaluating Internet Resources," on page 117, for one reproducible evaluation tool.

Taking a Process Approach to Research

The practice of working with information skills and assessing Web resources is often framed within a process approach to doing research projects. Several models exist for educators to integrate into their teaching and guide students as they undertake research tasks. For example, many teacher-librarians in British Columbia use "The Research Quest," based on a model developed by the British Columbia Teacher-librarian Association and adopted by the British Columbia Ministry of Education (**http://gladstone.vsb.bc.ca/library/research2.htm**). In the United States, Eisenberg and Berkowitz's Big6 is a popular information literacy model used to teach students and teachers how to find and assess information online. (See **http://www.big6.com/**.)

Other models include

- the 8Ws Information Literacy and Project-based Learning Model: **http://www.eduscapes.com/tap/topic71.htm**
- the Research Cycle by Jamie McKenzie from FNO.org: **http://www.fno.org/dec99/rcycle.html**
- Stripling and Pitts Research Process Model: **http://eduscapes.com/info/pitts.html**

Each information literacy model has its good points. Teachers are wise to examine and try out the different models and assess which one fits the particular needs in their classroom.

The demands for teachers to integrate ICTs into their students' learning have grown steadily for the past decade, and as a result, the pressure on teachers to become savvy technology users like many of their students has increased. With this knowledge, teachers can capitalize on students' interest in technology while teaching them essential information and technology skills. Just as they need a wide range of print resources for the classroom, teachers need to know which online resources will help students achieve required learning expectations. This need to know establishes a key connection to the school library program, where teacher-librarians use their knowledge and experience to find these resources and use them in information literacy. Just as they search for and evaluate traditional print resources, such as books and magazines, teacher-librarians apply that knowledge to online Web sites and work with classroom teachers to integrate this information into their literacy programs. Collaboration between classroom teachers and teacher-librarians enables students to learn the technical and critical thinking skills necessary to become fully literate.

8

Developing Literacy with Online Learning Environments

Martha Gabriel

Global classrooms, writers in electronic residence, virtual field trips, and WebQuests (learning activities based on using Internet resources) allow teachers and teacher-librarians to collaborate to foster communication, information sharing, and problem solving by children. Such interactive learning environments connect students globally and facilitate the use of the Internet for authentic learning activities.

This chapter outlines a variety of online learning environments that support information literacy and the new literacies; it also provides specific ideas that classroom teachers and teacher-librarians can act on to create digital learning experiences.

Online Learning Environments

In contrast to face-to-face learning environments, online learning environments use technology for one or more of these purposes: to let learners present specific information and readings, take part in discussions, collaborate with other students, and submit assignments.

New conceptions of student learning and the emergence of digital technologies have prompted educators to search for teaching and learning strategies that will meet learner needs. Integrating information literacy and the new literacies of information and communication technologies (ICT) into the curriculum has become a goal for literacy educators—documents by the International Reading Association (2001), International Society for Technology in Education (1998) and National Council of Teachers of English (1996) all reflect this. These carefully crafted standards, though, pose challenges for busy teachers, stretched to provide time and guidance for their students to accomplish all that is required. One effective solution is to integrate information literacy, the new literacies of ICT, *and* core curriculum standards as a means of "expanding time" within the classroom: this allows educators to achieve several learning outcomes within a single unit or activity.

Many educators recommend taking a constructivist approach to teaching. This approach builds on students' capacity to learn independently and to create their own understanding within a context. The teacher acts as a guide who organizes and facilitates learning experiences in the classroom. As J. Becker notes in *The Jossey-Bass Reader on Technology and Learning*, teachers who integrate this approach tend to view Web-based environments as relevant for teaching and learning activities in their classrooms (2000, pp. 80–111). The Internet has opened up the doors of individual classrooms to classrooms around the world. With an Internet connection and a computer in the classroom, students gain numerous learning opportunities that previously were inaccessible.

Classroom teachers and teacher-librarians have developed approaches to learning in Web-based environments. Online activities might focus on personal communication between students or classes; on collecting, sorting, and sharing data; or on solving a particular problem, which might involve collecting and analyzing data, developing creative solutions, and communicating those solutions to others (Harris, 1998, a, b). Interpersonal communication activities, seeking-accessing-and-analyzing activities, and problem-solving activities support the development of literacy skills in online environments. Students read text in many different forms, such as personal communications, hyperlinks, and images. They write text as they respond to keypal messages, jot down information in a word-processing file, or input their collected project data into a spreadsheet. Learners represent their ideas as they develop a presentation to share their discoveries with classmates, or work together to develop a class Web page.

Projects developed within online learning environments benefit from strong collaboration by the teacher-librarian and the classroom teacher. The classroom teacher brings an understanding of the core curriculum as well as the particular learning strengths and needs of the students to the partnership; the teacher-librarian brings expertise in information literacy and knowledge of appropriate online learning environments.

To better illustrate these applications, let us explore examples of authentic learning activities that focus on (1) interpersonal sharing, (2) seeking, collecting, and analyzing information, and (3) problem-solving.

Exploring Online Learning Environments

	Interpersonal Sharing	Information Collection and Analysis	Problem Solving
Benefits	• developing skills in proofreading • learning to reflect • valuing other perspectives	• skills in collecting and analyzing data • acceptance of responsibility for own learning • heightened global awareness	• investigation of essential questions • independent and collaborative work • real-life problems, real-life applications

Possible Challenges	• doing advance planning • finding suitable matches • sustaining interest and commitment to long-term project	• requirement for prior planning • timing of the project might not suit your classroom • consistent access to technology	• time challenges • registration fees • need to learn new technologies
Examples	• electronic keypals • global classroom exchanges • electronic appearances	• international challenge games • development of shared databases such as multicultural calendar • virtual field trips	• writing for publication • WebQuests • travel buddy projects

Interpersonal Sharing Activities

In these activities, individuals communicate electronically with other individuals or groups, or groups talk with other groups. These projects ordinarily involve communication between or among students in different geographic locations. Students might be engaged in an electronic keypals project, in which they correspond with students in another classroom. In global classrooms, there is interpersonal communication on a global level, with students communicating with learners in other countries. For example, if a teacher was reading *Zlata's Diary: A Child's Story of Sarajevo* to students, the teacher could develop a keypals project with a class of children living in Sarajevo.

To develop such a project, the teacher and the teacher-librarian should first decide whether the communication will be one-to-one or one-to-many. If one-to-one, the setup is similar to a traditional penpal activity, in which a student from one classroom is assigned the name of a student from a second classroom. These keypals write to one another and share personal information. A one-to-many activity involves the students from one classroom writing to students in another classroom, though the communication takes place through one file sent by the classroom teacher to the teacher in the other classroom.

Benefits for the Learners

These types of learning activities open up the walls of the classroom to children who live very different lives. They allow students in different classrooms to learn from one another, something that may be particularly important for students in areas with little diversity. When receiving messages from others, students learn to listen or read attentively, answer questions, and pose questions. They also learn the importance of proofreading their work and of reflecting before pressing the Send button. Students can come to value alternative points of view and different perspectives, which will assist them in better understanding their world. Communicating with and learning about other people via e-mail can also translate into continuous learning for students, as e-mail becomes one means of accessing information for lifelong learning.

Project Opportunities

Keypals and global classroom exchanges are two well-developed activities that allow students to communicate with others, on a one-to-one or on a one-to-many basis.

Intercultural E-mail Classroom Connections is one of the oldest and best-established keypal sites on the Internet. This site has served 21,000 teachers in 82 countries since 1992. The service has made classroom introductions for more than 220,000 participants. The technology used is either e-mail or **listserv**, an electronic communication tool in which members can send suggestions or ask questions to many people at the same time. The details of classroom exchanges, worked out by the participants, may centre on a theme or simply a sharing of information about the two classes.

http://iecc.org

Global classroom activities usually involve students from classrooms all over the world interacting with one another—either on a classroom-to-classroom basis, or as participants in a group event. The *Global SchoolNet* site hosts activities such as cyberfairs, an international learning challenge showcasing local communities for students and teachers from K to 12, and a registry listing more than 1,000 past and present interactive projects.

http://gsn.org

Another broker for classroom exchanges is the *ePALS Classroom*, set up in 1996. The ePALS site has facilitated numerous projects involving more than 100,000 classrooms in 191 countries. Project participants have an opportunity to share their questions, their cultures, and their stories online.

http://www.epals.com/projects

The *UNICEF Voices of Youth* is another international exchange in which students and their teachers have an opportunity to "speak with one another, and to explore different cultures in our global village." This site also provides information about the state of the world's children and children's rights.

http://unicef.org/voy

Learning circles are highly interactive, project-based partnerships among schools located throughout the globe. These cross-classroom collaborations allow teachers to team-teach with classroom teachers from around the world and students to work together with peers from a number of countries. The *Learning Circles* site provides a thorough introduction to the concept of learning circles, as well as information on joining a circle.

http://www.iearn.org/circles

Electronic appearances, by the "Women of NASA," for example, bring outside experts into classrooms. These guest appearances allow students to develop a better understanding of a topic or an area of endeavor from an expert in the field. Students who take part in these interactions may develop skills in interviewing online, thinking through questions, planning, and sharing information learned. The *Electronic Appearances* site includes a range of educational sites, including *Eyewitness to History* and *NASA Quest*.

http://webguide.enoreo.on.ca/projects/projectplanning/electronic.htm

At a number of sites on the Internet, students can pose questions and receive answers from subject experts. Teachers may choose to use these sites as places where students pose the questions that are stumping them. *Ask the Space Scientist* is an award-winning site which connects a subject expert in astronomy to learners.

http://image.gsfc.nasa.gov/poetry/ask/askmag.html

Possible Challenges

One challenge for classroom teachers and teacher-librarians is that a keypal or a global classroom project must be planned in advance. Teachers register with an organization and then plan their time accordingly. As well, some teachers have reported difficulty in finding a suitable match if they have a particular project in mind, such as sharing information about the watershed of their home area. The technology used for these exchanges does not always work—occasionally, classes have lost their e-mail messages and have had to start all over again.

The time frame for a communication project may also pose challenges for busy educators needing to complete work in various curriculum areas. If a keypal or global classroom project is envisioned as long term, it may be difficult for the classroom teachers to help students sustain their interest in, and commitment to, the project. Because most of the projects are run **asynchronously**—classes do not have to be online at the same time—time zones and geographical separation generally do *not* pose challenges for successful project completion.

Information Collection and Analysis Activities

Information collection and analysis activities involve students collecting, compiling, and comparing different types of factual information. Students frequently collect data locally and share it in a wider context. The data might be bird counts, road kill, or garbage on beaches. If a class is reading *Earthcycles and Ecosystems*, for instance, students might work on a local Earth Day project to help clean up the community beaches, and then share information about what they found on the World Wide Web. Students collect data and then post their information to an Internet-based database where it is shared with others.

To develop this type of information collection and analysis activity, the classroom teacher and the teacher-librarian should consult about what curricular area would have the greatest learning potential and interest for the students. When students take part in activities that they find meaningful, accelerated learning can take place. After the curricular area is chosen, the teachers need to register for the activity. Sometimes, a registration fee is required, making adequate advance planning and fund-raising necessary.

Benefits for Learners

When students do a collection activity, they learn skills in collecting and sorting data for genuine purposes, and in many projects, skills in working with one another to accomplish the activity's goals. They frequently have to plan their activity and work together to collect data. They come to learn that others in their group are depending on them to complete and share their work—this is one authentic way to help students learn to take responsibility for their learning. Students are responsible to their peers to finish what they committed to do; the audience for their learning is not solely their teacher.

In some projects, students learn how to use various programs in order to participate. For some challenges, students have to post their work using a word processor, while in other activities, students may have to learn to collect and analyze their data using a spreadsheet, and then learn how to post that information on the Web. Students learn how to compare data sets, using their own data and comparing it to the data posted by other classes. In many of these data collection and analysis activities, students also learn about another geographical area of the world. Students develop a heightened global awareness through their work.

Project Opportunities

A number of international challenges have been developed to engage the interest and research abilities of students and teachers. These projects allow students to collect data in their own community and share it with other participants. Eventually, a fairly complete database of information is developed through the participation of students and teachers.

GeoGame was developed by a classroom teacher in 1991. Its purpose is to increase awareness of cultural and geographical diversity. Classes that register online to participate are given a set of clues to follow. When they solve the clues and identify the geographical location, the students receive a certificate.

www.globalschoolhouse.org/project/gg/index.cfm

The GLOBE program, which is international, supports collaborative projects for K–12 students and educators. Students involved in GLOBE projects collect local data on topics such as soil, land covers, streams, and lakes, and report, graph, and share the data on the Internet. Participants can then compare, contrast, and discuss the rationale for the similarities and differences they discover.

http://www.globe.gov/globe_flash.html

Kidlink's Multicultural Calendar has been in existence since 1994. Students from around the world are invited to post information about their culture, holidays, and festivals. They can search entries by author, holiday, or country. They can also research and send new postings to the database.

www.kidlink.org/KIDPROJ/MCC/

Another approach to using the Internet for information collection and analysis activities is planning and carrying out a virtual field trip.

In one approach, a class of students goes on an actual field trip, then shares their progress and what they learned remotely with students in other classes. The *FRESH* Pilot project (Fieldtrip Resources Effectively SHared) in New Brunswick exemplified this approach. When students were on their field trip, they took digital photographs and movies and posted these on the Web to be shared with peers who went on the field trip virtually.

In a second approach to virtual fieldtrips, students in one geographic location post information about their own area and students in geographically remote classrooms access it. For example, the Creative Connections Project joins teachers and students in different parts of the world on a variety of field trips. In one trip, a group of students in Lijiang, Yunnan Province in China, shared their life, their culture, and a tour of their town with students in classes who had registered for the trip.

http://www.ccph.com/schools.html

In a third approach, teachers and students virtually accompany an adult or group of adults on an expedition, such as crossing the Arctic or visiting Mayan ruins. These field trips take place over a period of time, usually several months. Registered classes are able to communicate with the adventurers via e-mail or occasionally via video conferencing throughout the journey. One example is the *Antarctica: Scientific Journeys from McMurdo to the Pole* exploration. This site provides archived Webcasts and team field notes from a six-week exploration of Antarctica.

http://www.exploratorium.edu/origins/antarctica/index.html

Below are two other virtual field trip sites that provide further resources for educators looking for new possibilities to explore:

- *Field Trips Site:* **http://www.field-trips.org/vft/index.htm**
- *Virtual Field Trips Site:* **http://www.uen.org/utahlink/tours**

A final approach to taking a virtual field trip is to organize and conduct a field trip using Web sites such as museums. There are hundreds of sites with interactive virtual displays which can be matched to the curriculum outcomes chosen for a unit or theme.

The *Exploratarium* is the "museum of science, art and human perception." Teachers and students are able to access numerous interactive displays here, ranging from exploring the science of music to viewing the two rovers on Mars.

http://www.exploratorium.edu

The Franklin Institute is a museum of science which presents many hands-on exhibits for visitors who walk through the doors. The curators of *Franklin Institute Online* have developed many interactive exhibits for virtual visitors to enjoy, as well.

http://sln.fi.edu

The *Virtual Museum of Canada* is a gateway to myriad collections from Canadian museums. Exhibits in art, history, transportation, and science are included at this site, as well as a section for teachers—Learning with Museums.

http://www.virtualmuseum.ca

Possible Challenges

All these activities require prior planning on the part of the educators involved. For some of them, classes must register months in advance. These projects also tend to take some time to accomplish, so the time frame might be a challenge. Because the projects are generally organized by a central organization, they take place when the organizers decide they will, which may not be the best timing for individual classes and teachers. Finally, to complete the projects successfully, consistent access to technology is generally required, a difficulty in some jurisdictions.

Problem-Solving Activities

Problem-solving activities promote critical thinking, collaboration, and problem-based learning. In these activities, students collect, sort, and analyze information to solve a specific problem. Activities in which students develop pieces of writing and share them with mentors and peers online are also considered problem solving.

The classroom teacher in collaboration with the teacher-librarian can develop activities that are context specific and tied into a particular curriculum. For example, if a teacher is reading aloud *Daniel's Story* in the classroom, students could complete a problem-based activity on the Holocaust, available on the World Wide Web.

Benefits for Learners

When classroom work is based on solving problems, students may become very engaged in exploring possible answers. Students who work on solving particular problems sometimes work independently, a learning situation which has the potential to build self-esteem. Other types of problems require students to work in groups, where they learn that many perspectives on a problem may help solve that problem more quickly and efficiently. If carefully developed and chosen by teachers, the problems that students are working on can be drawn from real life and have specific applications in the real world. When investigating essential questions, students may learn science by doing science and by acting like scientists. Students may learn language arts by doing language arts, and becoming readers and writers. Pursuing essential questions also has the possibility of drawing in information from a multitude of areas to solve the problem. In *Beyond Technology*, Jamie McKenzie suggests, "questions and questioning may be the most powerful technologies of all" (2000, p. 1).

Project Suggestions

Electronic journals such as *MidLink Magazine* allow students to share their writing with their peers and see their own pieces in a public forum. *MidLink* has been publishing the work of students ages 8 to 18 online since 1994.

http://www.cs.ucf.edu/~MidLink

Writers in Electronic Residence provides a more focused writing environment for students and teachers. In this program, entire classes register for one term to work with an electronic writer in residence, and students receive feedback and encouragement on pieces of writing. Because of the intensity of the writing experience, there is a charge to participate in this very successful program.

http://ww.wier.ca

WebQuests provide an opportunity for learners to explore particular topics, to enter into simulations, and to engage in deep learning. The notion of WebQuests was developed by Bernie Dodge in the mid-1990s to facilitate exploring Web-based resources for authentic learning purposes. These resource-based activities make appropriate use of the World Wide Web for student learning. Teachers and teacher-librarians can develop their own WebQuests to reflect the curriculum and their own students' learning needs. They can also check out the hundreds of WebQuests available online; developed by teachers, these can be modified to suit particular curriculum and students.

http://webquest.sdsu.edu

Knowledge Forum is an online environment which facilitates the sharing of information and building of new information among students and teachers. Students communicate with one another and with teachers to pose questions, seek solutions, and share thinking and understandings.

http://www.knowledgeforum.com/K-12/products.htm

And finally, teachers and students in a number of different classrooms may work together on a travel buddy project.

In the *Vernon River School Anne of Green Gables World Tour*, an Anne of Green Gables doll from a school in Prince Edward Island was sent to Europe and to the United States to visit various classrooms before returning home. When Anne spent time in classrooms, students wrote journal entries about her adventures, and sent these on with Anne to the next group of student-hosts.

http://www.edu.pe.ca/vrcs/studentwork/2002/grade1/anne/anne.htm

The *Flat Stanley* project is a particular type of travel buddy project. Classes that have read and loved the Stanley books by Jeff Brown can register at a Web site to join a Flat Stanley project. (Stanley was flattened when a bulletin board fell on him and is now able to travel world-wide in an envelope or via e-mail.) Students share adventures with Stanley when he arrives in their classroom, write journals and take picture of the events, and then send Stanley on to the originating classroom, or to the next group of students in the ring.

http://flatstanley.enoreo.on.ca

Possible Challenges

Teachers may face a time challenge when they develop problem-solving projects. Some of the projects require classes to register, and others require a registration fee. It is sometimes difficult for teachers of younger children to find projects that are appropriate, yet challenging for their students. Occasionally, teachers and students have to learn how to use new technologies in order to participate in the problem-solving activity. And finally, educators may find that it is difficult to gain access to the technology when it is required for a particular problem-solving activity.

We have considered various online projects that focus on interpersonal sharing, information collection and analysis, and problem-solving. Adopting such projects allows classroom teachers and teacher-librarians to use online learning environments to support the core curriculum, information literacy initiatives, and the new literacies of ICT. All of the suggestions provided in this chapter can be implemented and coordinated by the classroom teacher and the teacher-librarian, and implemented on an individual classroom level. The education of literate citizens who are self-directed, lifelong learners is an essential goal for the 21st century—developing literacy and learning in online environments supports that important work.

9

Of course it's true! I found it on the Internet: Fostering Children's Online Critical Literacy

Keith McPherson

Critically literate Internet surfers have developed thinking skills that prevent them from being duped by online information and experiences.

Few educators would argue that our students' increased use of Web-based resources demands an increase in the development of their critical thinking skills. But just what do we mean by critical thinking skills, or critical literacy? For this chapter, **critical literacy** is defined as a person's ability to actively reflect upon and question the subjective nature of information and beliefs when making reasoned judgments and (if necessary) taking related actions. Such a definition draws heavily upon the social constructivist literacy theory proposed by P. Freire in *Education for Critical Consciousness.* The theory claims that the fostering of reflective language and thought "challenges the status quo in an effort to discover alternative paths for self and social development" (Shor, 1999). Essentially, critically literate Internet surfers have developed thinking skills that prevent them from being duped by online information and experiences; instead of giving the Internet power and control over their online experiences, they use their reasoning skills (the ability to determine the validity, credibility, and authenticity of information) to inform and control their Web-based explorations, decisions, and actions.

Teacher-librarians are no strangers to developing their student's critical literacy skills. For years they have developed tools and school library learning experiences aimed at helping students grapple with the construction and legitimacy of information in books, videos, television shows, posters, and more. These efforts continue today and have been expanded. They have become the backbone of a school's critical literacy program aimed at challenging the notion that "all information on the Web is true." In this chapter, we present practical instructional resources and examples that promote students' Web-based critical literacy skills.

The Need for Online Critical Literacy

"More than two thirds of school aged children retrieving information from the Internet do not check the information for credibility, reliability or authenticity."

—Media Awareness Network, 2001

The Internet has quickly become a resource that teachers and students turn to first. Studies by Ipsos and the Kaiser Family Foundation, both in 2003, report that 88 percent of Canadian and 96 percent of U.S. secondary students have either accessed the Internet for research or for enjoyment. Also, the number of schools connected to the Internet is now 80 percent in Canada and 99 percent in the United States (see Statistics Canada, 2002; National Center for Educational Statistics, 2002). Contributing factors may be government initiatives to improve school Internet access, the

- stereotyping
- violence
- online hate
- unethical views
- harassment
- unreliable information
- invasion of privacy
- pornography
- online crime
- false arguments

estimated 45 billion Web sites from which to find online information (Zakon, 2004), and the dramatic decrease in computer prices.

Unfortunately, a 2001 study from the Media Awareness Network indicates that more than two-thirds of school-aged children do not check Internet information for credibility, reliability, or authenticity; it also reports that one-third of secondary students believe that all Internet information is true. These assumptions and uncritical Web-surfing practices have serious implications when a student accesses Web sites containing "challenging information," such as sophisticated advertising, negative or destructive values, and incorrect information (see list at left). The need to develop students' skills in authenticating Internet content is a great impetus for educators to work with online information experts, like the teacher-librarian.

Authenticating Internet Site Information

North American teacher-librarians have been developing children's abilities to authenticate resources for decades. **Authenticating**, or the ability to discern fact from fiction, is a theme fully developed across most K–12 curricula. (Unlike resource assessment, which is aimed at determining the overall value or significance of a resource, resource authentication is focused specifically on proving a resource's genuineness or authority.) Nowhere, though, is the ability to determine the truth more essential than in the "wilds" of the Internet. Educators often ask these two questions about authenticating Internet sites:

- "When should teachers begin developing students' online critical literacy?"
- "How do we teach students how to authenticate Internet information?"

The time to start is now, and the younger the better. In *Growing Up Wired*, the Kaiser Family Foundation reported that by 2003, 70 percent of children were coming to school familiar with using computers and 91 percent were watching two or more hours of television a day. This high exposure to screen media at such an early age indicates that educators can never start too early in developing children's ability to discern truth from deception.

Fortunately, there are many resources to aid educators in this endeavor. The following pages present three examples of K–12 classroom activities used by teacher-librarians working with teachers in developing students' abilities to authenticate online materials.

Authenticating Online Information in the Early Elementary Classroom

Most early elementary students are more likely to be learning to read and write printed text at school than learning to critically evaluate Internet sites. Nevertheless, as experienced teacher-librarians know, their Internet critical thinking skills can be developed early through a variety of non-Internet activities and materials. The development of young children's ability to discern fact from fiction can be accomplished by

- comparing and contrasting fiction and information books
- developing concepts of real and make-believe in narratives
- using drama to explore the difference between imagination and reality
- comparing real and make-believe objects, animals, and so on
- sorting what is real and not real on a video, DVD, television program, or piece of clip art

Picture book narratives with stark contrasts between make-believe and reality:

Clever Cat by Peter Collington

Where the Wild Things Are by Maurice Sendack

How I Became a Pirate by Melinda Long

Sector 7 by David Weisner

A Bad Case of Stripes by David Shannon

Developing Concepts of Real and Make-Believe

The following activity is an example of how teacher-librarians use picture books to further develop children's concept of reality and make-believe. I recommend using narratives to begin this exploration because most early elementary children (and probably more important, educators) are familiar and comfortable with print resources.

Clever Cat, by Peter Collington, is an illustrated narrative well suited to helping young children begin sorting concepts of reality and make-believe (more examples are listed in the margin). The story recounts the hilarious adventures of a cat, named Mr. Tibs, who decides to quit being a "dumb" cat and live more like a human being. Children will easily see when Mr. Tibs stops acting like any real cat they have ever witnessed.

First, the teacher reads *Clever Cat* to the whole group. Using chart paper with a "T-chart" drawn on it, the teacher initiates a whole-group brainstorming and sorting of Mr. Tibs's actions into categories that remind them of a real cat or a make-believe cat.

Real Cat	Make-believe Cat
• sleeps	• uses credit card
• waits for mice	• shops
• catches mice	• uses can opener
• catches birds	• goes to movies
• eats	• plays tennis

Children are encouraged to reflect upon what they have seen, heard, and felt a real cat do when determining the reality of Mr. Tibs's actions. The teacher might create a third column titled "not sure" if the children are unsure if his actions fit in either category. Early primary students can sort illustrations of Mr. Tibs's activities; later primary groups can sort text. In small groups or individually, students draw their own "T charts" on paper and finish sorting Mr. Tibs's actions. At this stage, the teacher can easily observe and assist students struggling to sort Mr. Tibs's actions into real or make-believe categories.

To reinforce concepts of reality and make-believe, it is wise to repeat this sorting activity for a variety of narratives where the character or plot shifts through obvious states of reality and make-believe. Some children have difficulties determining if a narrative context or character is real—for example, the Tooth Fairy and Santa—so the concepts of reality and make-believe should be revisited frequently throughout the year. Ways to successfully reinforce these concepts at the early elementary level are listed below.

Tips for Separating Reality and Make-Believe in Picture Books

Do not rush students through sorting process.

Encourage student talk when negotiating reality and make-believe.

Link the reality of characters' actions with students' sensory experiences.

Repeat this activity using several illustrated narratives.

Always provide a space on the page for "not sure" or "both" items.

Reinforce concepts of reality and make-believe throughout the year.

Have K–1 students sort images of reality and make-believe.

Once primary students are comfortable in determining reality and make-believe in narratives, teachers and teacher-librarians can encourage them to determine the reality (truths) or make-believe (deceptions) in resources, such as drama and videos. At the same time, these students can view and sort digital Internet images and animations into real, make-believe, and not sure categories. Examples of Web sites containing primary-level images of real and make-believe subjects are

- *Sesame Street:* **www.sesamestreet.com**
- *Blue's Clues:* **www.nickjr.com/home/shows/blue/index.html**

The thrust of these activities is twofold. First, they serve to begin developing young children's awareness that they cannot always assume that information is true or real—an understanding essential to their current and future online explorations. Second, they demonstrate the mentoring role of the teacher-librarian in introducing and reinforcing concepts of authenticity to and with both students and classroom teachers.

Authenticating Online Information in the Upper Elementary Classroom

This activity could be used in a Grades 6 to 8 Social Studies unit aimed at assisting students in identifying racial stereotypes in online information. It explores the degrees in which online and print newspapers can use racial stereotypes to distort a crime report's truth. It is adapted from a lesson plan titled "Perceptions of Race and Crime" by J. Talim, for the Media Awareness Network.

Begin by displaying the Urban Alliance of Race Relations photo. Talim suggests asking students, "What is the message of this public service campaign? What stereotypes and assumptions does this ad rely on? From where do we get these beliefs? How does this ad counteract them? Is this an effective ad? Why or why not?" The intent of these questions is to initiate discussions on the use of racial stereotypes to substantiate one's argument.

Urban Alliance on Race Relations anti-racism poster located at **http://www.media-awareness.ca/ english/resources/educational/ overheads/crime/ policeman_psa.cfm**

Next, write the following crime news headlines and reports on the chalkboard:

- Detectives describe man fleeing crime site as a 30-year-old Latino male.
- Black woman questioned in red light district murder.
- Police mourn loss of fellow officer slain by Asian street racers.

Discuss with the students what is similar about all three reports. Ask, "Is it necessary to mention a criminal's race? What are reporters trying to

Major Online North American Newspapers

USA Today
www.usatoday.com/

New York Times
www.nytimes.com/

Globe and Mail
www.globeandmail.com/

Los Angeles Times
www.latimes.com/

Boston Globe
http://www.boston.com/news/globe/

National Post
www.nationalpost.com

CNN
edition.cnn.com/US/

do by mentioning a criminal's race? Does changing the criminal's culture or skin color affect the report? Why or why not? One sure way to identify if racism is in a news report is to replace the culture or skin color of the criminal with that of the mainstream culture in our community. Does this change the intention of the message?"

Note: If your class requires more activities to heighten their awareness of stereotypes in crime reports, see "Perceptions of Race and Crime," by J. Talim, Media Awareness Network (2004). It can be accessed at **http://www.media-awareness.ca/english/resources/educational/lessons/secondary/crime/race_and_crime.cfm.**

Have students work in groups of two or three to search and print off a variety of crime reports from both online and offline (printed newspaper) news sources (see the list of online newspaper resources in the margin). The searching and analysis of reports should be spread over a week or two, research should go back in time one month, and each group should collect at least 20 unique online and 20 unique offline crime reports. Using the compare/contrast chart below, students then analyze and sort the online reports according to racial identification: (1) None, (2) Relevant, and (3) Unnecessary.

None	Relevant	Unnecessary

The numbers of articles for each column can be graphed for each online newspaper as well. Next, have the students use the T-chart to sort, compare, and contrast the types of racial identification in printed newspaper crime reports. Prompt the class to discuss the types of racial identification noted in crime reports in general and how online newspapers can be encouraged to report crime ethically. Are there differences between online and offline newspaper reporting?

Letters to the editor or posters could develop from students' findings; alternatively, the class could be encouraged to compare trends in racial identification in news reports with clips or transcripts of TV news reports.

Authenticating Online Information in the High School Classroom

Most 14- to 18-year-old students are learning to be independent and proficient when searching Web resources for school projects; however, if not taught some key critical thinking tools and procedures, students may report fraudulent Internet information as the truth. This activity introduces Grades 8 to 12 students to the concept of Web page duplicity and presents a tool for revealing Web site spoofs and impostors.

Display the Web site addresses listed below, and ask students to predict which of the URL extensions—.org, .biz, .edu, .gov, .info, .net—would most likely link to the "real" United States of America White House Web page. Ask students to rank the sites from (1) the most likely to be the page to (6) the least likely. Ask students to explain why they ranked some pages more likely to be the real White House homepage over others. Using a list of common domain extensions, ask students to try to define each extension and discuss how an URL's extension adds to understanding of a Web site's content. Have students visit **www.whois.sc**. This is one of several domain name search engines that retrieves Web site content information. Students then key in each of the White House URLs and retrieve the site's vital statistics. Note that the description for **www.whitehouse.net** indicates that the site is a "Spoof on the formalities of the White House and its inhabitants" and the description for **www.whitehouse.gov** is "the official web site for the White House and President W. Bush, the 43rd President of the United States." Have students enter each URL into the "Whois Source" search engine to check the description of the remaining White House URLs to determine each site's agenda.

Which one of these URLs points to the official White House page of the United States of America?

www.whitehouse.org	www.whitehouse.gov
www.whitehouse.biz	www.whitehouse.info
www.whitehouse.edu	www.whitehouse.net

Common Domain Extensions

.org non-commercial organizations
.biz business organizations
.com commercial organizations
.edu educational organizations
.gov government
.info information organizations
.net network-related companies

The many U.S. White House–like Web sites offer educators one of the most fertile grounds for developing their students' ability to use domain name search engines; however, several Canadian and international examples can also provide practice.

For example, students may visit **http://paulmartintime.ca/** and **http://pm.gc.ca** to determine which site presents the official views of Canadian Prime Minister Paul Martin. Note that, in this case, the Whois search results in domain information that does not clearly state which site is official and which satirical. Students can enter the owner's contact information to conduct a Google search and begin determining whose perspectives are behind each of the Web sites.

Another example is to have students use the **www.whois.sc** domain search engine to determine which of the following URL extensions—**.va**, **.ca**, **.it**, **.us**, **.com**, **.net**, **.org**, **.info**, **.biz**, and **.us**—is the authentic Vatican Web site.

Web Site Resources Focused on Developing Students' Online Critical Literacy

A quick visit to any of the following Web site spoofs will help illustrate the enormous efforts Web page designers will go to when developing perceived authenticity into their sites.

- **www.thehammer.ca** (Satire of print and online Canadian and international news)
- **www.golfcross.com** (New Zealand site promoting elliptical golf balls)
- **www.theonion.com** (Political satire of print and online U.S. and international news)
- **http://www.improb.com/airchives/classical/cat/cat.html** (Research that suggests felines have an aversion to bearded men)
- **http://www.dhmo.org/** (Research-based site selling the benefits of the chemical H_2O).
- **http://www.lakelandschools.org/EDTECH/webdetechtor/ SaveThePacificNorthwestTreeOctopus.htm** (A site dedicated to saving the Pacific Northwest Coast tree octopus—complete with clear photographs).

A visit to one or more of these sites also helps illustrate the wide variety of techniques and tools that Web page designers employ in an effort to build authenticity.

The activities presented in this chapter are only three examples of many that teacher-librarians employ in an effort to help K–12 students become aware of these techniques, as well as giving students their own tools for determining whether a Web site is authentic or not. The following list of online resources and instructional tools is aimed at helping teachers and teacher-librarians in nurturing a set of diverse online critical literacy skills that complement and go well beyond those presented in this chapter.

Web Sites for Developing Children's Online Critical Literacy

Early Elementary

Surfing safely on the Internet:
http://www.siec.k12.in.us/~west/proj/surf/surfless.htm

Teaching TV:
http://www.media-awareness.ca/english/resources/ educational/lessons/elementary/television_radio/ teaching_tv_storytelling.cfm

Elementary

The Internet Detective:
http://sosig.ac.uk/desire/internet-detective.html

Quality Information Checklist:
http://www.quick.org.uk/menu.htm

Jim Kaoun's Five Criteria for Evaluating Web Pages:
http://www.library.cornell.edu/olinuris/ref/webcrit.html

For Educators

Evaluating Web Pages (Widner University):
http://www2.widener.edu/Wolfgram-Memorial-Library/ webevaluation/examples.htm

Kathy Schrock's Online Evaluation:
http://school.discovery.com/schrockguide/eval.html

Trinity College, Evaluating Websites:
http://library.trinity.wa.edu.au/library/study/evaluating.htm

Media Awareness Network:
http://www.media-awareness.ca/english/teachers/index.cfm

The suggested practical activities and Web sites given in this chapter illustrate how authenticating online information can be taught as early as Kindergarten and honed into a keen skill by graduation in Grade 12. Authenticating information, though, is only one critical thinking skill needed. Examples of other online critical thinking skills include

- *making ethical uses of information.* In this case, students are encouraged to reflect upon their online understandings and make decisions and take actions that seek to make the world a better place to live. For example, writing letters to national/local representatives with suggestions for sharing wealth and resources.
- *determining false arguments.* An exploration of the site *Truth, Honesty, and Justice* (**http://www.truth-and-justice.info/spinwar.html**) will help students become more aware of politicians' ability to weave false arguments in an effort to persuade their electorates.
- *"reading" advertising.* A review of spoofs on common advertisements (see **http://www.adbusters.org/spoofads/**) helps students understand social stereotypes and the promotion of negative social values.
- *recognizing bias.* Comparing and contrasting Jon Scieszka's *The True Story of the Three Little Pigs* with the original "Three Little Pigs" provides students with experiences in recognizing perspective, stereotypes, and bias in newspaper and political reports.

Fortunately, most schools have an expert in their midst—the teacher-librarian—who is trained to work with classroom teachers and students in developing these, and many other, critical literacies.

Planning Guide

Grade Level: _____ Number of Students: _____ Date: _____

Teacher(s): _____ Teacher-Librarian: _____

Theme or Topic: (Curriculum connections)

Timeline: (Number of classes, schedule of sessions)

Specific Learning Outcomes: (Refer to provincial or state guides.)

Assessing the Learning: (Tools to be used, timing of assessments, who does what)

Learning Resources:

Learning Activities:

Criteria For Evaluating Internet Resources

Source: Adapted from the Internet Resource Evaluation Criteria (Resource Sheet 12) — School Libraries in Canada 2001, Vol. 20, No. 4. The Ethics of Information Use

Name: _____

URL: http:// _____

Title: _____

Criterion	Yes	No	Why
Authority Is it clear who is responsible for the contents of the page? (organization's name) Is there a way of verifying the legitimacy of the page's sponsor? (phone number, address, something other than e-mail address?) Is it clear who wrote the material and are the author's qualifications clearly stated? Is the material protected by copyright and is the copyright holder named?			
Accuracy Are the sources for any factual information clearly listed so they can be verified? Is the material free of grammatical, spelling, and typographical errors? Is it clear who has the responsibility for the accuracy of the content of the material? If charts or graphs are included, are they clearly labeled and easy to read? Is the information valuable and/or appropriate to your task?			

Criterion	Yes	No	Why
Objectivity or Bias Does the site rely on loaded language or broad, unsubstantiated statements? Is emotion used as a means of persuasion? Does the site offer more than one viewpoint? Are there links to other or alternative viewpoints?			
Currency Are there dates on the page to indicate • when the page was written? • when the page was first placed on the Web? • when the page was last revised? Are there any other indications that the material is kept current? If graphs or charts are included, is it clearly stated when the data were gathered?			
Coverage Does the information presented seem to be complete? Is the information consistent with what you already know or have found in other sources? Does the site include a paragraph that explains what its purpose is? (to entertain, explain, advertise, persuade, or inform) Are there links to other sites to support or enhance the information presented?			

Professional Resources

Books

Armstrong, Tricia. 2000. *Information Transformation: Teaching Strategies for Authentic Research, Projects and Activities.* Markham, ON: Pembroke.

Baxter, Kathleen, A., and Marcia Agnes Kochel. 1999. *Gotcha! Nonfiction Booktalks to Get Kids Excited about Reading.* Westport, CT: Libraries Unlimited.

Burniske, R. 2000. *Literacy in the Cyberage.* Newark, DE: International Reading Association.

Cramer, Eugene H., and Marrietta Castle, eds. 1994. *Fostering the Love of Reading: The Affective Domain in Reading Education.* Newark, DE: International Reading Association.

Daniels, Harvey. 1994. *Literature Circles.* Portland, ME: Stenhouse.

Gregory, Kathleen, Caren Cameron, and Anne Davies. 1997. *Setting and Using Criteria.* Winnipeg, MB: Peguis.

Harada, V., and J. Yoshian. 2005. *Assessing Learning: Librarians and Teachers as Partners.* Portsmouth, NH: Libraries Unlimited.

Harvey, Stephanie. 1998. *Nonfiction Matters: Reading, Writing and Research in Grades 3–8.* Portland, ME: Stenhouse.

Harvey, Stephanie, and Anne Goudvis. 2000. *Strategies That Work.* Portland, ME: Stenhouse.

Hyerle, David. 1996. *Visual Tools for Constructing Knowledge.* Alexandria, VA: Association for Supervision and Curriculum Development.

Jobe, Ron, and Mary Dayton-Sakari. 2004. *Info-Kids: How to Use Non-fiction to Turn Reluctant Readers into Enthusiastic Learners.* Markham, ON: Pembroke Publishers.

Knowles, Elizabeth, and Martha Smith. 2001. *Reading Rules!* Westport, CT: Libraries Unlimited.

Koechlin, Carol, and Sandi Zwaan. 1997. *Teaching Tools for the Information Age.* Markham, ON: Pembroke.

Koechlin, Carol, and Sandi Zwaan. 2001. *Info Tasks for Successful Learning.* Markham, ON: Pembroke.

Moline, Steve. 1995. *I See What You Mean: Children at Work with Visual Information K–8.* Portland, ME: Stenhouse.

Morgan, Nora, and Juliana Saxton. 1994. *Asking Better Questions: Models, Techniques and Classroom Activities for Engaging Students in Learning.* Markham, ON: Pembroke.

Moss, Joy F., and Marilyn F. Fenster. 2002. *From Literature to Literacy: Bridging Learning in the Library and the Primary Grade Classroom.* Newark, DE: International Reading Association.

Parry, Terence, and Gayle Gregory. 1998. *Designing Brain Compatible Learning.* Arlington Heights: Skylight.

Schwartz, Linda, and Kathlene Willing. 2001. *Computer Activities for the Cooperative Classroom.* Markham, ON: Pembroke.

Thomas, N. 2004. *Information Literacy and Information Skills Instruction: Applying Research to Practice in the School Library Media Centre.* 2nd edition. San Jose, CA: Libraries Unlimited.

Turner, P., and A. Reidling. 2003. *Helping Teachers Teach: A School Library Media Specialist's Role.* 3rd edition. Portsmouth, NH: Libraries Unlimited.

Vasquez, V., et al. 2003. *Getting beyond "I like the book": Creating Space for Critical Literacy in K–6 Classrooms.* Newark, DE: International Reading Association.

Wilhelm, Jeffery D., and Paul Freidemann, with Julie Erickson. 1998. *Hyperlearning: Where Projects, Inquiry, and Research Meet.* Portland, ME: Stenhouse.

Zarnowski, Myra, Richard M. Kerper, and Julie M. Jensen, eds. 2001. *The Best in Children's Nonfiction: Reading, Writing and Teaching Orbis Pictus Award Books.* Urbana, IL: National Council of Teachers of English.

Web Sites

American Association of School Librarians: http://www.ala.org/aasl/

Debbie Abilock Curriculum Site: http://nueveaschool.org/~debbie/library/overview.html

From Now On—The Educational Technology, by Jamie McKenzie: http://www.fno.org

The Graphic Organizer: http://www.graphic.org/

Jigsaw Classroom: http://www.jigsaw.org/

Kathy Schrock's Guide for Educators: http://school.discovery.com/schrockguide/index.html

Media Awareness Network: http://www.media-awareness.ca/

References

Chapter 1

American Library Association Presidential Committee on Information Literacy. (1989). Final report. (ERIC Document Reproduction Service No. ED 315074). Retrieved March 23, 2004, from http://www.infolit.org/documents/89Report.htm.

Asselin, M. (2005). Preparing preservice teachers as members of the information literate school community. In J. Henri & M. Asselin (Eds.), *The information literate school community: Leadership issues* (pp. 187–202). Wagga Wagga, Australia: Centre for Information Studies, Charles Sturt University.

Asselin, M. (2000). Poised for change: Effects of a teacher education project on preservice teachers' knowledge of the school library program and role of the teacher-librarian. *School Libraries Worldwide, 6*(2), 72–87.

Asselin, M., & Doiron, R. (2003). An analysis of the inclusion of school library programs and services in the preparation of preservice teachers in Canadian universities. *Behavioral and Social Sciences Librarian 22*(1), 19–32.

Asselin, M., Oberg, D., & Branch, J. (Eds.). (2003). *Achieving information literacy: Standards for school libraries in Canada*. Ottawa, ON: Canadian Library Association.

Association of College and Research Libraries. (1998). A progress report on information literacy: An update on the American Library Association Presidential Committee on Information Literacy: Final Report. Retrieved January 6, 2004, from http://www.ala.org/acrl/nili/nili.html.

Council of Ministers of Education, Canada. (1999). Shared priorities in education at the dawn of the 21st century: Future directions for the Council of Ministers of Education, Canada. Retrieved January 27, 2003, from http://www.cmec.ca/reports/victoria99.en.stm.

Doiron, R., & Davies, J. (1998). *Partners in learning: Students, teachers, and the school library*. Englewood, CO: Libraries Unlimited.

Elley, W. B. (1992). *How in the world do students read?* The Hague: International Association for the Evaluation of Educational Achievement.

Froese, V. (1997). The relationship of school materials and resources to reading literacy: An international perspective. In L. Lighthall and K. Haycock (Eds.), *Information rich but knowledge poor? Emerging issues for schools and libraries worldwide* (pp. 283–303). Seattle, WA: International Association of Teacher-librarianship.

Haycock, K. (2003). *The crisis in Canada's school libraries: The case for reform and re-investment*. Toronto: Association of Canadian Publishers and the Department of Canadian Heritage. Retrieved March 4, 2004, from http://www.peopleforeducation.com/librarycoalition/Report03.pdf.

International Reading Association. (1999). *Providing books and other print materials for classroom and school libraries*. Retrieved March 2, 2004, from http://www.ira.org/positions/media_center.html.

International Reading Association. (2000). In support of credentialed library media professionals in school library media centers. Retrieved March 2, 2004, from http://www.ira.org/positions/cre_libra.html.

Iowa Association of Teacher-librarians. (n.d.) School library media studies on achievement. Retrieved March 1, 2004, from http://www.iema-ia.org/IEMA119.html.

Kinzer, C. K., & Leander, K. (2003). Technology and the language arts: Implications of an expanded definition of literacy. In J. Flood, D. Lapp, J. Squire, & J. Jensen (Eds.), *Handbook of research on teaching the English Language Arts*, 2nd ed. (pp. 546–565). Mahwah, NJ: Lawrence Erlbaum.

Lance, K. C. (2001). Proof of the power: Recent research on the impact of school library media programs on the academic achievement of U.S. public school students. ERIC Digest. Retrieved February 28, 2004, from http://www.ericfacility.net/ericdigests/ed456861.html.

Lance, K. C., Welborn, L., & Hamilton-Pennell, C. (1993). *The impact of school library media centers on academic achievement*. Castle Rock, CO: Willow Research and Publishing.

Leu, D. J., Jr., Kinzer, C. K., Coiro, J., & Cammack, D. W. (2004). Toward a theory of new literacies emerging from the Internet and other information and communication technologies. In R. B. Ruddell & N. Unrau (Eds.), *Theoretical models and processes of reading*, 5th ed. (pp. 1570–1613). Newark, DE: International Reading Association. Retrieved March 1, 2004, from http://www.readingonline.org/newliteracies/lit_index.asp?HREF=leu/.

Leu, D. J. (2002). The new literacies: Research on reading instruction with the Internet and other digital technologies. In S. J. Samuels and A. E. Farstrup (Eds.), *What research has to say about reading instruction* (pp. 310–336). Newark, DE: International Reading Association.

Lonsdale, M. *Impact of school libraries on student achievement: A review of the research*. Retrieved March 1, 2004, from http://www.asla.org.au/research/index.htm.

Ministry of Education, Government of British Columbia. (2000). *The critical skills required of the Canadian workforce*. Retrieved February 28, 2004, from www.bced.gov.bc.ca/careers/planning/work/critskll.htm.

Moore, P. (2000). Primary school children's interaction with library media. *Teacher Librarian, 27*, 7–11.

Morrow, L. M. (1998). Motivating lifelong voluntary readers. Unpublished manuscript. New Brunswick, NJ: Rutgers University. Cited in International Reading Association, 1999, *In support of credentialed library media professionals in school library media centers*. Retrieved March 2, 2004, from http://www.ira.org/positions/cre_libra.html.

Neumann, S. (2001). *The role of school libraries in elementary and secondary education*. Retrieved January 16, 2004, from http://www.imls.gov/pubs/whitehouse0602/neuman.htm.

Neumann, S., Celano, D., Greco, A., & Shue, P. (2001). *Access for all: Closing the book gap for children in early education*. Newark, DE: International Reading Association.

Ohio Educational Media Association. (2004). *Student learning through Ohio school libraries: The Ohio Research Study*. Retrieved March 1, 2004, from http://www.oelma.org/studentlearning/default.asp.

Ohio Educational Library Media Association. (2004). *Student learning through Ohio school libraries: The students' voices*. Retrieved March 1, 2004, from http://www.oelma.org/StudentLearning/documents/OELMADoc2.pdf.

Ontario Library Association. (1999). *Information studies: Curriculum for schools and school libraries*. Toronto: Ontario School Library Association.

Prince Edward Island Department of Education. (2001). *Building information literacy: Strategies for developing informed decision makers and life long learners*. Retrieved January 4, 2004, from http://www.edu.pe.ca/bil/.

Reading Today. (February–March 2004). Libraries called key. Retrieved February 28, 2004, from http://www.ira.org/publications/rty/0402_libraries.html.

Rodney, M. J., Lance, K. C., & Hamilton-Pennell, C. (2002). *Make the connection: Quality school library media programs impact academic achievement in Iowa*. Bettendorf, IA: Mississippi Bend Area Education Agency.

Smith, E. G. (2001). *Texas school libraries: Standards, resources, services, and students' performance*. [Texas]: EGS Research & Consulting for Texas State Library and Archives Commission. Retrieved February 12, 2004, from http://www.tsl.state.tx.us/ld/pubs/schlibsurvey/index.html.

Topping, K., et al. (2003). Policy and practice implications of the Program for International Student Assessment (PISA) 2000: Report of the International Reading Association PISA Task Force. Retrieved June 20, 2003, from http://www.reading.org/advocacy/pisa.pdf.

Washington Library Media Association. (1996). *Essential skills for information literacy: Benchmarks for information literacy*. Retrieved January 4, 2004, from http://www.wlma.org/Instruction/benchmarks.htm.

Whelan, D. L. (2003). Why isn't information literacy catching on? *School Library Journal*. Retrieved January 22, 2004, from http://slj.reviewsnews.com/index.asp?layout=article&articleid=CA318993&publication=slj.

Zweizig, D. L., & Hopkins, D. M. (1999). *Lessons from Library Power. Enriching teaching and learning*. An Initiative of the DeWitt Wallace-Reader's Digest Fund. Englewood, CO: Libraries Unlimited.

Chapter 2

Asselin, M., Oberg, D., & Branch, J. (Eds.). (2003). *Achieving information literacy: Standards for school libraries in Canada*. Ottawa, ON: Canadian Library Association.

Brown, C. (2004). America's most wanted: Teachers who collaborate. *Teacher Librarian 32*, 13–18.

Doiron, R., & Davies, J. (1998). *Partners in learning: Students, teachers, and the school library*. Englewood, CO: Libraries Unlimited.

Chapter 3

Doiron, R., & Davies, J. (1996). *Partners in learning: Students, teachers and the school library*. Englewood, CO: Libraries Unlimited.

Keifer, B. (Feb. 2001). Understanding reading. *School Library Journal, 47*(2), 48–53.

Krashen, S. (Dec. 1997/Jan. 1999). Bridging inequity with books. *Educational Leadership, 55*(4), 18–22.

Krashen, S. (1993). *The power of reading: Insights from the research*. Englewood, CO: Libraries Unlimited.

Lance, K. C. (2002). Proof of the power: Recent research on the impact of school library media programs on the academic achievement of U.S. public school students. *Information and Technology*. 1–12. Retrieved June 11, 2004, from ERIC database. (ED456861).

Lance, K. C., Hamilton-Pennell, C., & Rodney, M. J. (1999). *Information empowered: The school librarian as an agent of academic achievement in Alaska schools*. Juneau, AK: Alaska State Library.

Lance, K. C., Welborn, L., & Hamilton-Pennell, C. (1993). *The impact of school library media centers on academic achievement*. Castle Rock, CO: Hi Willow Research and Publishing.

Lonsdale, M. (2003). *Impact of school libraries on student achievement: A review of the research*. Retrieved January 19, 2005, from http://www.asla.org.au/research/index.html.

Plucker, J. A., Humphrey, J., Kearns, A. M., & Walter, C. N. (2002). *Improving school libraries and independent reading: 1997–2002 Impact evaluation of the K–12 school library printed materials grant*. Policy Issue Report R-2002-02. Bloomington, IN: Education Policy Center. ERIC document ED467648.

Staton, M. (Sept./Oct. 98). Reading motivation: The librarian's role in helping teachers develop programs that work. *Library Talk, 11*(4), 18–21.

Stead, T. (2002). *Is that a fact? Teaching nonfiction writing in K–3*. Markham, ON: Pembroke.

Chapter 4

Adams, M., Bell, L., & Griffin, P. (Eds.). (1997). *Teaching for diversity and social justice: A sourcebook*. New York: Routledge.

Berman, S. (1997). *Children's social consciousness and the development of social responsibility*. New York: State University of New York Press.

Clyde, A. L. (2005). Policy, social justice, and information literature school community. In J. Henri & M. Asselin (Eds.), *The information literate school community 2: Issues of leadership* (pp. 92–104). Wagga Wagga, Australia: Centre for Information Studies.

Our School/Ourselves. A quarterly journal devoted to issues of social justice and education in Canada. See http://www.policyalternatives.ca/index.cfm?act=main&call=A5671525.

Paley, V. (1984). *Boys and girls: Superheroes in the doll corner*. Chicago: University of Chicago Press.

Rethinking Schools Online. Web site of an organization committed to equity and to the vision that public education is central to the creation of a humane, multiracial democracy. See http://www.rethinkingschools.org/.

Chapter 5

California Department of Education. (1996). *Teaching reading: A balanced, comprehensive approach to teaching reading in prekindergarten through grade three*. Sacramento, CA: http://goldmine.cde.ca.gov/.

Clay, Marie M. (1989). Concepts about print in English and other languages. *Reading Teacher, 42*(4), 268–276.

Dickinson, D., and Smith, M. (1994). Long-term effects of preschool teachers' book readings on low-income children's vocabulary and story comprehension. *Reading Research Quarterly, 29*, 104–122.

Doiron, R. (Ed.). (1999). *Role of the teacher-librarian: A handbook for administrators*. Retrieved March 18, 2004, from http://www.upei.ca/~fac_ed/projects/handbook/librarin.htm.

Duke, N. K. (2000). 3.6 minutes a day: The scarcity of informational texts in first grade. *Reading Research Quarterly, 35*(2), 202–224.

Filipenko, M. J. (2003). Constructing word/world knowledge together: Young children's emerging understandings of/with informational texts. Unpublished doctoral dissertation. Vancouver: The University of British Columbia.

Gunning, T. G. (2000). *Creating literacy instruction for all children*. Needham Heights, MA: Allyn & Bacon.

Holdaway, D. (1979). *The foundations of literacy*. Sydney, Australia: Ashton Scholastic.

Labbo, L. D., & Teale, W. H. (1997). An emergent-literacy perspective on reading instruction in kindergarten. In S. A. Stahl & D. A. Hayes (Eds.), *Instructional models in reading* (pp. 249–283). Mahwah, NJ: Lawrence Erlbaum Associates.

Pappas, C. C. (1991). Fostering full access to literacy by including information books. *Language Arts, 68*, 449–462.

Pappas, C. C. (1993). Is narrative "primary"? Some insights from kindergartens' pretend readings of stories and information books. *Journal of Reading Behaviour, 25*(1), 97–127.

Piccolo, J. A. (1987). Expository text structure: Teaching and learning strategies. *The Reading Teacher, 40*, 838–847.

Purcell-Gates, Victoria. (1989). What oral/written language differences can tell us about beginning instruction. *Reading Teacher, 42*(4), 290–294.

Richgels, E. S., McGee, J. M., & Slaton, E. A. (1989). Teaching expository text structure in reading and writing. In K. D. Muth (Ed.), *Children's comprehension of text* (pp. 167–184). Newark, DE: International Reading Association.

Salinger, T. S. (1996). *Literacy for young children*. Englewood, NJ: Prentice Hall.

Chapter 6

American Association of School Librarians and the Association for Educational Communications and Technology. (1998). *Information power: Building partnerships for power*. Chicago: American Library Association.

American Association of School Librarians. (1999). *Information literacy: A position paper on information problem solving*. Retrieved March 21, 2000, from http://www.ala.org/aasl/positions/ps_inforlit.html.

Bereiter, C., & Scardamelia, M. (1987). *The psychology of written composition*. Hillsdale, NJ: Erlbaum.

Berkowitz, S. J. (1986). Effects of instruction in text organization on sixth graders' memory for expository reading. *Reading Research Quarterly, 20*(2), 161–178.

Bloom, B. S. (Ed.). (1956). *Taxonomy of educational objectives: The classification of educational goals. Handbook 1: Cognitive domain*. New York: David McKay.

Chall, J. S., Jacobs, V. A., & Baldwin, L. E. (1990). *The reading crisis: Why poor children fall behind*. Cambridge, MA: Harvard University Press.

Eisenberg, M. B., & Berkowitz, R. E. (1999). *The new improved Big6 workshop handbook*. Worthington, OH: Linworth Publishing.

Harvey, S., and Goudvis, A. (2000). *Strategies that work: Teaching comprehension to enhance understanding*. Markham, ON: Pembroke Publishers.

Hidi, S., & Anderson,V. (1987). Providing written summaries: Task demands, cognitive operations, and implications for instruction. *Reviewing Educational Research*, 56, 473–493.

Hirsch, E. D. (2003). Reading comprehension requires knowledge of words and the world: Scientific insights into the fourth-grade slump and the nation's stagnant reading comprehension scores. *American Educator*, 27(1), 10–22, 28–29, 48.

Lee, E. A. (2005). Remembering the basics: Reading and the information literate school/community. In J. Henri & M. Asselin (Eds.), *The information literate school community 2: Issues of leadership* (pp. 65–78). Walla Walla, Australia: Centre for Information Studies, Charles Sturt University.

National Reading Panel. (2000). *Teaching children to read: An evidence-based assessment of the scientific research literature on reading and its implications for reading instruction*. Washington, D.C.: National Institute of Child Health and Human Development.

Ontario School Library Association. (1996). *Position statement on school library information centres and teacher librarians*. Retrieved July 27, 2005, from http://www.accessola.com/osla/advocacy.htm.

Ontario School Library Association. (1999). *Information Studies Kindergarten to Grade 12*. Toronto: Ontario Library Association.

Pressley, M. (1998). *Reading instruction that works: The case for balanced teaching*. New York: The Guilford Press.

Pressley, M., Johnson, C. J., Symons, S., McGoldrick, J., & Kurita, J. A. (1989). Strategies that improve children's memory and comprehension of what is read. *Elementary School Journal*, 89, 3–32.

Raphael, T. E. (1986). Teaching question–answer relationships, revisited. *The Reading Teacher*, 39, 516–522.

School District No. 44 (North Vancouver). (1999). *Reading 44: A core reading framework—Secondary*. p. 138.

Taylor, B. M. (1982). Text structure and children's comprehension and memory for expository material. *Journal of Educational Psychology*, 74(3), 323–340.

The Big Six Associates, LLC. (2003). Retrieved on April 9, 2004, from http://www.big6.com/showarticle.php?id=415.

Vacca, R. T., & Vacca, J. L. (1999). *Content area reading: Literacy and learning across the curriculum* (6th ed.). New York: Longman.

Chapter 7

American Association of School Librarians and the Association for Educational Communications and Technology. (1998). *Information power: Building partnerships for learning*. Chicago: American Library Association.

Berners-Lee, Tim. (2004). The worldwide web browser. Retrieved November 25, 2004, from http://www.w3.org/People/Berners-Lee/WorldWideWeb.html.

Bowman, David. (2004). Thinking through the technology puzzle. *From Now On 14(1)*. Retrieved December 5, 2004, from http://www.fno.org/oct04/integrating.html.

Bright Planet. (2004). *Part 4: Boolean Basic*. Retrieved August 30, 2005, from http://www.brightplanet.com/deepcontent/tutorials/search/part4.asp.

CASL, ATLC. (2003). *Achieving information literacy: Standards for school library programs in Canada*. Ottawa, ON: Canadian Library Association.

Dublin Core Metadata Initiative. (2004). *DCMI Metadata Terms*. Retrieved August 29, 2005, from http://dublincore.org/documents/dcmi-terms/.

Eisenberg, Mike, & Berkowitz, Bob. (2004). *Big6: An information problem-solving process*. Retrieved November 30, 2004, from http://www.big6.com/.

Illinois Mathematics and Science Academy. (2002). *How fast is the Web growing?* Retrieved November 25, 2004, from http://21cif.imsa.edu/inform/totw/tip6/growth.html.

Internet World Statistics. (2004). *World Internet usage and population statistics*. Retrieved November 25, 2004, from http://www.internetworldstats.com/stats.htm.

NASBE. (2003). *Teacher's use of Technology*, Summer 11(3). Retrieved November 30, 2004, from http://www.nasbe.org/Educational_Issues/Policy_Updates/11_3.html.

Schrock, Kathy. (2002). *The ABC's of website evaluation*. Retrieved December 5, 2004, from http://school.discovery.com/schrockguide/eval.html.

Statistics Canada. (2004). *Connectivity and learning in Canada's schools*. Retrieved August 29, 2005, from http://www.statcan.ca/english/research/56F0004MIE/56F0004MIE2004011.pdf.

W3Schools. (2004). *XML Tutorial*. Retrieved August 30, 2005, from http://www.w3schools.com/xml/default.asp.

Chapter 8

American Library Association and Association for Educational Communications and Technology. (1998). Information power: The nine information literacy standards for student learning. In *Information power: Building partnerships for learning*. Retrieved February 1, 2004, from http://www.ala.org.

Becker, J. (2000). Internet use by teachers. In *The Jossey-Bass reader on technology and learning*. (pp. 80–111). San Francisco, CA: Jossey-Bass.

Dede, C. (1995). The evolution of constructivist learning environments: Immersion in distributed, virtual worlds. *Educational Technology*, 35(5), 46–52.

Harris, J. (1998a). Curriculum-based telecollaboration: Using activity structures to design student projects. *Learning and Leading with Technology, 26*(1), 6–15.

Harris, J. (1998b). Virtual architecture's web home. Retrieved March 15, 2004, from http://virtual-architecture.wm.edu/.

International Reading Association Board of Directors. (2001). *Integrating literacy and technology in the curriculum.* Retrieved February 4, 2004, from http://www.reading.org/positions.

International Society for Technology in Education. (1998). *National educational technology standards for students.* Retrieved February 1, 2004, from http://cnets.iste.org/students/s_stands.html.

Jonassen, D. H. (2000). *Computers as mindtools for schools.* Columbus, OH: Merrill.

Leu, D. J., Jr. (2001, March). Internet project: Preparing students for new literacies in a global village [Exploring Literacy on the Internet department]. *The Reading Teacher, 54*(6). Retrieved March 15, 2004, from http://www.readingonline.org/electronic/elec_index.asp?HREF=/electronic/RT/3-01_Column/index.html.

McKenzie, J. (2000). *Beyond technology: Questioning, research and the information literate school.* Bellingham, WA: FNO Press.

National Council of Teachers of English & the International Reading Association. (1996). *Standards for the English language arts.* Retrieved March 15, 2004, from http://www.ncte.org/print.asp?id=110846&node=204.

Scardamalia, M., & Bereiter, C. (2000). Engaging students in a knowledge society. In *The Jossey-Bass reader on technology and learning.* (pp. 312–319). San Francisco, CA: Jossey-Bass.

National Center for Educational Statistics. (2002). *Internet access in U.S. public schools and classrooms: 1994–2002.* Retrieved March 1, 2005, from http://nces.ed.gov/surveys/frss/publications/2004011/2.asp.

Shor, I. (1999). What is critical literacy? *Journal of Pedagogy, Pluralism, and Practice, 4*(1). Retrieved March 1, 2005, from Lesley College, Cambridge, MA, Web site: http://www.lesley.edu/journals/jppp/4/shor.html.

Statistics Canada. (2002). *The Daily: Computer access at school and at home.* Retrieved March 1, 2005, from http://www.statcan.ca/Daily/English/021029/d021029a.htm.

Talim, J. (2004). Perceptions of race and crime. *Media awareness network.* Retrieved March 1, 2005, from http://www.media-awareness.ca/english/resources/secondary/Perceptions_of_Race_and_Crime_Lesson.htmphoto.cfmphoto.html.

U.S. Department of Education. (2004). *Assistive Technology Program.* Retrieved March 1, 2005, from http://www.ed.gov/about/reports/annual/2001report/edlite-345.html.

Zakon, R. H. (2004). *Hobbes' Internet Timeline v7.0.* Retrieved March 1, 2005, from http://www.zakon.org/robert/internet/timeline/.

Chapter 9

Case, R. (2005). *Making critical thinking an integral part of electronic research.* Retrieved March 1, 2005, from School District #38, Richmond, British Columbia, at http://www.sd38.bc.ca:8004/~TC2/making.

Freire, P. (1973). *Education for critical consciousness.* New York: Seabury.

Industry Canada. (2004). *Computers for schools.* Retrieved March 1, 2005, from http://cfs-ope.ic.gc.ca/Default.asp?lang=en.

Ipsos. (2003). *The Internet is changing the way Canadians socialize.* Retrieved March 1, 2005, from http://www.ipsos-na.com/news/pressrelease.cfm?id=2008.

Kaiser Family Foundation. (2003). *Growing up wired: Survey on youth and the Internet in the Silicon Valley.* Retrieved March 1, 2005, from http://www.kff.org/entmedia/loader.cfm?url=/commonspot/security/getfile.cfm&PageID=14232.

Media Awareness Network. (2001a). *Young Canadians in a wired world survey.* Retrieved March 1, 2005, from http://www.media-awareness.ca/english/special_initiatives/surveys/index.cfm.

Index